"Just as the flapping
of a butterfly's wings
can effect climate changes
on the other side of the planet
our happiness
can affect attitude changes
on the other side of the planet."

~ Gayleen Williams

The Happiness Toolkit

Happy Readers

"The bottom line is what everyone really wants is HAPPINESS! They think they want money, houses, cars, careers, relationships and all the rest – but they only want these things because they believe it will make them happiness easily and effortlessly with "THE HAPPINESS TOOLKIT" Read it TODAY and be HAPPY NOW!"

~ Dr. Robert Anthony, Professional Coach and Author of over 15 books published in 22 countries, including "The Ultimate Secrets of Total Self-Confidence," which continues to be a best seller after being in publication for almost 30 years. (DrRobertAnthony.com)

"This positive, upbeat book is full of great ways to be happier and more effective in every area of your life!"

~ Brian Tracy has helped over 5 million people achieve their goals as the author of numerous best-selling books and programs. (BrianTracy.com)

"If you want to live a happier life full of energy and purpose, then read and re-read this incredible book! Gayleen Williams' words will inspire you to live your dreams!" ~ James Malinchak, Co-author "Chicken Soup for the College Soul" (malinchak.com)

"Everyone is looking for happiness. In fact, it's the most sought after commodity in the world. People try to find it through their families and significant relationships, their careers, their religious or spiritual affiliations, sex, vacations, hobbies, cars, money, and addictions, and the list goes on and on. Gayleen's book provides life-changing keys one can apply to move away from their dramas, and find real happiness." ~ Jim Britt, Author of numerous best-selling books and programs (JimBritt.com)

"In the end, isn't that what life's about? To be happy? Otherwise, what is it for? THANK YOU GAYLEEN! for giving us these core concepts to having a life that is worthwhile and fulfilling. Awesome!" ~ Lynn Rose, International Speaker/Singer/Author/TV & Radio Host and Creator "The Wow Factor," and "The Goal Getter Experience" (LynnRose.com)

"Gayleen is a living testament of the power that 'choosing happiness' has luminous effects in one's life. Her very countenance mirrors the sheer beauty of her internal joy. I am grateful such a woman took the time and energy to transcribe her thoughts and experiences into a book in a manner that makes the notion of 'choosing to be happy' a simple concept for all to understand. The real life stories contained throughout are entertaining and thought provoking, as at every turn, your mind shifts to thinking of the 'choices' we have made in the past... And gives fodder to how we will choose to decide to make the 'choice to be happy' in our daily encounters and situations for the future. Clearly, we are reminded that as adults we have a 'chance to live in joy' as productive and caring individuals... This book will certainly help the reader learn how to live a full and happy life regardless of what twists and bends life may present." ~ Joni Rae Rogers-Kante, Chairman, CEO & Founder SeneGence International

"Some people believe happiness is elusive, some feel it's unattainable, but now Gayleen Williams has not only made it attainable; she's given you the step-by-step process to live your happiest life starting today with "THE HAPPINESS TOOLKIT" ~ Lynn Pierce, Founder Women's Business Empowerment Summit; Author "Breakthrough to Success and 19 Keys to Mastering Every Area of Your Life" (LynnPierce.com)

"What a great book! I feel like I'm having a conversation with a non-judgmental and unconditionally loving mentor. Inside the pages lie some golden keys to being happy and ultimately contented with life in this world as a human being. The Happiness Tools are easy and fun and rewarding – I'm sure many people will benefit from the tools in this informative, entertaining book." ~ Deberra O'Brien, Principal & Interior Designer/Project Manager of Avenue Real Estate & Development, Inc

"There is wisdom on every page of this book! People who read it will be rich in happiness." ~ Irwin Zucker, President Promotion in Motion Public Relations; Founder Book Publicist Club Southern California (PromotionInMotion.net)

"The most wonderful aspect of this book is that it is everyday practical, usable and easy to understand. I am certain that if you use the concepts and tools, you will find greater happiness and satisfaction in your life!"~ Patricia Clason, Co-author "Speaking of Success" and Director, Center for Creative Learning (patriciaclason.com)

"I am so glad you have put your tools for maintaining happiness in a book form. Having known you for years, I have long admired your ability to stay happy in spite of life's challenges. I'm sure many people will benefit from reading it." ~ Elaine Vener, CEO Vener Management

"Your book looks great. I enjoyed the section on humor ... I would love to meet you in person!!!"
~ Roberta Gold, R.T.C., Secretary, the Association for Applied and Therapeutic Humor (laf4u.com)

"Gayleen Williams and her Co-Author Linda Hancock Moore have

written a compassionate and practical book that is a 'kit for happiness.' She has aligned with other great thinkers in a brilliant, practical, step-by-step format, which is easy to understand, believe and practice. What follows for the reader is greater happiness in his or her life and relationships, as well as other rewards. By way of practicing the wisdom of this very informative book new clarity is created, which heals old wounds and directs us toward new insights." ~ Reverend Dr. Les Turner & Reverend Audrey Turner, Creative Center for Spiritual Living

"Congratulations on the book's completion. It was well worth the time... to create an exceptional work – tools on how we can achieve happiness." ~ Carol Latham, President, Fashion Event Productions

"Gayleen Williams exemplifies her book!" ~ John Delavalle, Speech Therapist aka John Mayo, Actor

"What a powerful book – full of tools to use, complete with instructions that are easy to follow."
~ Karen Grace Mangini, Dog Behaviorist (TheBowWowMethod.com)

"THE HAPPINESS TOOLKIT is a rich compendium of quotations, spiritual and philosophical insights, positive statements, everyday wisdom for information and applied life enhancement, especially for counselors, coaches, teachers and parents for use in guiding teens and young adults." ~ Dr. Peggy Holmes, Minister and Author of Radical Technology for Personal Growth

"It's a good book – especially for people who don't feel good about themselves. They say life is an inside job and this book will help people." ~ Anna Bogdanovich, 15-year-old Student

"This book will help you reconcile you present with your past, which will make you feel the energy of a well balanced happy life." ~ Miguel Rivera, Vice President, Bank Branch Manager

"Congratulations on completing the book ... The matter of being content is often difficult to explain as it seems to conjure up lack of ambition in people's minds. I am particularly impressed and inspired by how you explained that – how we enslave ourselves by our wants, desires and lust for things we do not have, rather than spending more time being content with what we have. I started hopping through the book ... and I kept finding meaningful things, maybe expressed previously, but seemingly new and fresh because it is expressed in a different way. Wonderful work." ~ Lindsay Latham, Writer

"I love this book! It's very friendly. I stole it from a friend and will not give it back!
~ Joanne Paratore, Recording Artist/Producer/Composer/Singer/Songwriter/Arranger

"I personally believe that everyone from heads of state to shut-ins should read THE HAPPINESS TOOLKIT... The book has ideas that are easy to follow and easy to share ... I love it!" ~ Linda Lee Grau, Producer/Host radio show "Talent in the Southland"

"Your book is fabulous! I am so grateful for THE HAPPINESS TOOLKIT. Having so many wonderful words of wisdom and well-being affirmations collected in one easy to read book is exquisite. This book has helped me get in touch with my own personal happiness; thank you for that! If one thought provoking affirmation doesn't get you thinking, another one will; you can count on it! Thank you for contributing to my happiness."
~ Tod Spence, President of the Board of Directors, Unity Long Beach

"Gayleen lives the world she offers to others."
~ Lenny Johnson

"Gayleen and I have grown, laughed, and cultivated an enduring friendship together. It is an honor and pure delight to see Gayleen realize this milestone and accomplishment in her life, to see the many new glorious rewards of Karma for a job well done continuing to bless this inspirational soul. Gayleen's playful nature and intellect radiates from every turn of every page. Enjoy living your happiest and brightest life! Enjoy Gayleen! Enjoy this book!"
~ Marisa Stewart, Producer, Consultant (MSWKP.com)

"I watched this book develop as this author friend rose above extreme difficulties thrown in her path. Not only did she prevail past, philosophize and later laugh, she carried our hearts and minds along. She truly is a walking example of using her happiness tools. Have her book within reach when your heart misses something or someone. Her words will inspire, encourage and teach you to be your happiest." ~ Kay Reul, Actress and Artist (artistkay.com)

"I like the ideas you have put out there. You have some poignant points and helpful insight... Thank you again for writing such a hopeful and inspirational book... your ideas are wonderful." ~ Joan Chen, UCLA student

"Gayleen gives us all the tools to achieve happiness. The book is well-presented, filled with wonderful and appropriate quotes and is easy to follow and understand. It's truly a great guide for anyone seeking happiness in their life." ~ John Chancellor, Mentor/Coach, Author of "Lessons in Life" (teachthesoul.com)

"THE HAPPINESS TOOLKIT can be used on multiple levels: as a how-to manual, daily lessons to put into action, or as a great textbook for classes. In reading this book, I realized my consciousness was in need of a major tune-up. Thank you for my new beginning. It is a great recovery program to emerge from negativity and into a new world of being creative, constructive, healthy and happy. You can open nearly any page and therein is a great lesson. Our culture is decades overdue for this work of genius. There's more than enough in it to last a lifetime. I love Gayleen's state of consciousness."

~ Reverend John Levy, Creative Center for Spiritual Living

Gayleen Williams with Linda Hancock Moore

Publikshed by:

TABLE OF CONTENTS

The Happiness Toolkit

Author: Gayleen Williams
Co-author: Linda Hancock Moore
Copy Editor: Marisa Stewart
Cover Design: Gayleen Williams
Publisher: **Butterfly Publications 800-890-8996**
ButterflyPublications.com
Email: support@ButterflyPublications.com
Printed in the United States - ISBN print ed. 978-1-892644-31-2

The Happiness Toolkit

TABLE OF CONTENTS

TABLE OF CONTENTS

TABLE OF CONTENTS

The Happiness Toolkit

FOREWORD

Dear Reader:

This book purports to contain twenty-one (21) "Actions" to promote and construct happiness; the state of that all too frequent elusive feeling of well being in the life of the consummate health reader. *Joie de vivre* as a universal fountain of youth for many, if not most of us, is often right at our fingertips although we fail to recognize it.

This treatise is far more than a set of cute gimmicks designed to appeal to the uninitiated. It cites solid research studies documented in the psychological literature in order to buttress its mandates and suggestions that can and do work if, and when, assiduously applied. *As a man thinketh in his heart so is he* is an old aphorism that has stood the test of time.

We can do just what we want to do but frequently fail to do at our own peril. The suggestion for relaxation advocated by Dr. Herbert Benson at the Harvard School and cited by the author in this book is merely one of many notable procedures designed to eventuate in happiness. The subject is simply asked to stretch out in a relaxed position while slowly repeating the word "ONE" along with deep abdominal breathing. It works and ought to be employed as a daily procedure for the rest of one's life. Although good to begin the day, it can be used virtually anywhere at any time thereafter.

The putative erudite reader who may tend to impugn such mundane and simplistic "happiness tools" with maledictory comments ex cathedra would do well to try some of these actions themselves. They could be in for a big surprise.

FOREWORD

It is indeed an unabridged pleasure for me to write a few laudatory words as a Foreword for this virtually indispensable treatise on happiness and health for anyone.

Dr. Calvin J. Frederick. ABPP, ABPH, FACP
Professor, Department of Psychiatry and Biobehavioral Sciences
University of California Los Angeles School of Medicine

Dr. Frederick has had a long and prestigious career, including serving on the faculty of George Washington University Medical School, Johns Hopkins University Medical School, the National Institute of Mental Health and the World Federation of Mental Health. He has been a keynote speaker and a professional reviewer numerous times and a consultant to governmental agencies along with major corporations. Utilizing his expertise in disaster assistance, emergency mental health, crime and delinquency, suicide prevention and radiation effects he has appeared on television and in court over 300 times as an expert witness, as well as a hostage negotiator.

The Happiness Toolkit

PREFACE

It must be true that happiness is like the butterfly, elusive. It seems that only seven-percent (7%) of people are truly happy! This is according to respected Gallup who surveyed people in 105 countries. I find this statistic appalling, especially since I believe that people can learn to be happier.

I wasn't always the happy woman I am now. Coming from a background of poverty, dysfunction and even sexual abuse, I spent many years feeling unhappy, discouraged, overwhelmed and exhausted. It was important for me to find how to be happier.

After 20+ years of research and applying these tools I now share with you I was able to capture the elusive butterfly and build a happy life. Not only did I get happy I now stay happy almost all the time! You, too, can get happy and stay happy!

Now, imagine if your happiness you could make those around you happier, too. Well, it seems it does. **It seems our happiness has an effect on the happiness of those around us, and their happiness in turn affects those around them**. Yes, also according to Gallup, if someone has a happy friend, their chances of being happy go up 5%, and if your friend has another happy friend, their chances go up another 10%, bringing this happy fact to a 25-30% increase exponentially. Just knowing this makes me happy!

Please note that as with any toolkit you can pick whatever tool you may need at any given time. The premise of this book is that if you are the best person you can be you will be your happiest. So, if you find you want to improve your skill of forgiveness use that tool. If you find you could improve your skill of sticking to something or if you find you have trouble making a decision then use the tool that applies to each of those. You get the idea... ☺.

Paul Erlich wrote, "The flapping of a butterfly's wings can cause changes in the climate on the other side of the planet." This has became known as "The Butterfly Effect." Enjoy the following explanation by Wikipedia.

THE BUTTERFLY EFFECT

(As explained by Wikipedia)

> In 1961, Lorenz was using a numerical computer model to rerun a weather prediction, when, as a shortcut on a number in the sequence, he entered the decimal .506 instead of entering the full .506127 the computer would hold. The result was a completely different weather scenario. Lorenz published his findings in a 1963 paper for the New York Academy of Sciences noting that, "One meteorologist remarked that if the theory were correct, one flap of a seagull's wings could change the course of weather forever." Later speeches and papers by Lorenz used the more poetic butterfly. According to Lorenz, upon failing to provide a title for a talk he was to present at in 1972 for the American Association for the Advancement of Science, Philip Merilees concocted "Does the flap of a butterfly's wings in Brazil set off a tornado in Texas?" as a title. Although a butterfly flapping its wings has remained constant in the expression of this concept, the location of the butterfly, the consequences, and the location of the consequences have varied widely.
>
> The phrase refers to the idea a butterfly's wings might create tiny changes in the atmosphere that may ultimately alter the path of a tornado or delay, accelerate or even prevent the occurrence of a tornado in a certain location. The flapping wing represents a small change in the initial condition of the system, which causes a chain of events leading to large-scale alterations of events (compare: domino effect). While the butterfly does not "cause" the tornado in the sense of

> providing the energy for the tornado, it does "cause" it in the sense that the flap of its wings is an essential part of the initial condition resulting in a tornado, and without that flap that particular tornado would not have existed.

Therefore, like the butterfly's wings in Paul Erlich's expression, "The flapping of a butterfly's wing can cause changes in the climate of the other side of the planet," our happiness can cause changes on the other side of the planet.

Moreover, I believe that just as butterfly wings flapping can change the climate on the other side of the planet, words can change hearts and minds and, therefore, lives. Hence, this book.

Butterflies have a special significance for me. When I was 17, my mother wrote a poem about me being a butterfly, "with wings so strong they could lift you to the sky and yet so fragile they will flake in your fingertips." (You can find a copy in the dedication section – it's truly beautiful.)

Butterflies are associated with transformation, new beginnings, freedom and happiness. As elusive as happiness, like the butterfly is, I finally discovered effective Happiness Action Tools™ that helped me transform into the butterfly my mother saw me as being.

Even now, I use these tools regularly to get happy and stay happy! Now I am sharing them, so that you can be your happiest, and your friends can be their happiest, and their friends can be their happiest, and on and on as the flapping of the butterfly wings go. ☺

I believe the words of my mother's poem fit each of us. We are all fragile and yet, stronger in more ways than we can imagine. My goal is to inspire you to become the best person you can be so you can be your very happiest. Go catch that elusive butterfly so you, too, can get happy and stay happy!

PART 1

Building the Foundation

Just as a solid foundation builds a solid house,
a solid foundation will help you build your happiest life
so you GET HAPPY and STAY HAPPY!

Gayleen's Basic Philosophies

- *Self-esteem is the basis of a happy life and is learned, both consciously and unconsciously.*
- *Our happiness is dependent upon what we believe.*
- *Belief systems are decisions we make and accept as a "script," usually as a child, often based on experiences with limited or faulty information.*
- *Ideas and thoughts predicate decisions. By creating new thoughts we change our beliefs and, therefore, change our belief systems or "scripts."*
- *Our belief systems determine our expectations.*
- *We get exactly what we expect in life not what we want, not what we hope for or what we affirm, but what we really feel worthy of.*
- *Positive Expectation Statements™ (which other people call Affirmations) repeated often enough, will change our belief systems so we manifest positive results.*
- *Our perceptions are totally our own. Absolutely no one shares our perception or views life exactly as we do, simply because we each have our own individual experiences and existence.*
- *Happiness is a state of consciousness. We are the happiest when we have a sense of well-being, which is most often not about money or material possessions.*
- *Happiness is living from peace and joy; it is living without fear. Fear is the main thing, if not the only thing, that holds us back in life. We are fearful when we do not love ourselves. When we have healthy self-love, we trust ourselves and our participation in the universe and the process of life. The truth is that we cannot be fearful and trust at the same time. If we are trusting we are not fearful. The way that we trust is by living our best life, which enhances our self-esteem. From this comes happiness and a life that is not only good for us, but a better life for all we touch.*

INTRODUCTION

Anyone Can Be Happy

"Employ your time in improving yourself
by other men's writings,
so that you shall gain easily what others have labored hard for."
~ Socrates

"All truly wise thoughts have been thought already
thousands of times; but to make them truly ours,
we must think them over again honestly,
till they take root in our personal experience."
~ Johann Wolfgang von Goethe

Wouldn't you like to capture the elusive butterfly? Wouldn't you like to be in the be in that seven-percent (7%)? Wouldn't you like to have a sense of well-being, feel energized and enthusiastic almost every day? What if you could feel the way Cathryn (Mrs. Tommy) Franks, put it, "This is the life... this life was more than I ever knew to dream about."

You can! I am sharing how I got happier so you can do that for yourself – and do it more easily and quicker than I did. As I said, during my many years of research, I discovered 21 powerful Happiness Action Tools™ that helped me go from being a shy, frightened, insecure, unhappy little girl to a self-assured woman who is happy most of the time, no matter what the circumstances are.

Asked How I Changed My Life

People began asking me how I went from being that fearful little girl to the self-confident happy woman I am now. Some often comment I must have led a carefree life to be so happy now. One of my friends answers that with, "Anything but!"

It is worth understanding that I am not speaking from hypothetical theory, but share my message based on actual experience. You can find an autobiography of much of my life at TheHappinessCommunity.com. It's a touching story, however much of it is sad, and I have decided it's not necessary or appropriate for a book on happiness.

It's true; my life was full of heartaches, disappointments, and difficult challenges. Yet, now I am happier than I ever could have imagined. Since it became important for me to find a way to be happier, I have done extensive research, studied, gone through counseling and learned from experience.

You can learn and benefit from my journey to achieving greater happiness in life. I want to save you at least some of the time and effort it took me, so you can more quickly find your own happiness.

Limiting Beliefs

Much of the unhappiness in life stems from people having so little self-esteem they don't believe they have a right to be happy. I have a lot of company in believing self-esteem, or the lack of it, comes from belief systems that we adopt as children and live from the rest of our life. This quote by Dennis Prager, host of the radio show THE HAPPINESS HOUR, ties in well here, "We not only have a right to be happy, we have an obligation to be happy, because our happiness has an effect on everyone around us."

Psychologists call these belief systems "scripts" or "tapes." Unfortunately, these belief systems often come from limited, sometimes erroneous, information, which is why they are often referred to as "limiting beliefs."

Whatever you want to call them it is worth noting that too often these scripts, tapes or belief systems affect our every decision, and by doing that, limit the possibilities of our being the most we can be, and knowing happiness to its fullest. **These belief systems become the driving force behind much of what we do in our life.**

Recognizing and changing our "script" *is* possible. Spawned by a decision I made as a child, from just one childhood episode, my script influenced almost every decision I made from then on – until I discovered it and changed it. I recognize now that because of it, I created the "mistaken certainty" in my mind that, "I did not deserve to have what I really wanted in life." This completion of this book is the proof that we can change our script.

I now believe I am worthy of getting what I want. I am happier now and because of that so are many other people. It is now my mission to make as many people happy as I can.

We all experience temporary sadness or other unhappy emotions. Truth is we will all go through challenging times. Yet, now I know we can overcome them and get to times of happiness again. Furthermore, you will be happier more of the time, and your times of being down will be shorter by using these happiness action tools. "Keep your copy close at hand knowing you now have words that will inspire, encourage and teach you to be your happiest," suggests Kay Reul.

Our Brain is Like a Computer

Our brain is very much like a computer. As such, it does not know the difference between fact and fiction. Input determines output. Our brain simply acts on whatever we put in it. The good news is we have decision-making capabilities that the computer does not have. We can choose to change, choose to think differently, and choose a different response, and this all begins to happen when we change the input.

John F. Kennedy believed (and I agree with him) that, "Man is still the most extraordinary computer of all." This is not to say I think of myself, or anyone, as simply a computer. We are much more complicated beings than that. We have emotions coming from what, I believe, is a soul or spirit giving us religious and/or spiritual beliefs. I have that in my life, too, profoundly.

Many people would certainly benefit by listening to their higher power, which could help in changing the input to their "computer." I merely liken the mind to a computer, and the "garbage in; garbage out" concept, or in our case, good thoughts in; better life created.

I found enlightenment and direction through the wise wordsmiths of the ages; brilliant people who I believe each had their own connections to that loving, supportive higher source. Moreover, in re-programming "my computer" with these wise thoughts, getting happy and staying happy is easier and easier.

Famed Actress Goldie Hawn, now recognized as a "Happiness Expert," has started a non-profit organization to help children develop happier, healthier lives. She pointed out, "So maybe that's what the difference is, that when you intend to be happy, then you figure out ways to sustain your happiness or your ability to feel moments of joy in your life."

Children don't think of themselves as the butterfly in Paul Erlich's quote, or in Lorenz's research. Still the flapping of the wings starts at each life's beginning and continues, either out of belief in life and it's possibilities, or in desperation to survive. We often feel like a caterpillar crawling along, not realizing that we can transform our lives and become a beautiful butterfly.

As Max Ehrmann, in his poem DESIDERATA said, "Everyone has his story." My life surely has not been as horrible as some lives, still it was bad enough to confirm the miracle of my rising above it and give me the inspiration to share what I learned. You can empower yourself by my research into finding greater happiness. I didn't emerge from my cocoon overnight. It took years for me to seek out truths and discover the Actions that would set the butterfly in me free.

With the wisdom in what I read and heard, I became empowered by healthier thoughts and so my self-love and self-esteem grew over time. I have put what I learned into this book so you can benefit from it and live your happiest life.

Wisdom Lives Forever

Learning is benefiting from other people's experience and learning. Degrees prove that people have studied and, therefore, learned. Thomas Mann said, "We are not free, separate, and independent entities, but like links in a chain, and we could not by any means be what we are without those who went before us and showed us the way."

What we learn from the wise and articulate is invaluable. I also learned from my own life experience. It became important to help others discover their purpose and confidence; to find both their child within and the part of them that can be the wise and loving parent to themselves they might not have had.

I affectionately refer to myself as an "information junkie." I love to learn. I satiate my hunger for knowledge with wonderful information from great, learned people. I have earned many certifications (see ABOUT THE AUTHOR), even if not a traditional college degree. I'm sure I'd qualify for many college degrees based on my life experiences.

Yet, my proudest "degree" is one I've given myself: the degree in happiness achievement. If you feel you deserve your own degree in happiness achievement, visit TheHappinessCommunity.com and print out a certificate suitable for framing.

If you like quotes, as I do, there are over 550 of them herein! I use them to lend my ideas credibility and augment your learning experience. These expressions from other people can enhance your understanding of my concepts; expressions from people who perhaps are famous and/or who have articulated them in perhaps more beautiful and powerful ways.

Encouraged By Friends

My brother, David, encouraged me for many years to finish this, so I finally decided to ask a few friends to encourage me also. I got a lot of encouragement. However, Linda Grau took the time to show her belief in me by putting her reasons in writing. Her letter to me is brilliant and I use it often as inspiration. Here's an excerpt:

> "The store of knowledge that you have about casting off disadvantages, hurts and adverse circumstances is uniquely yours. However, parts of the disadvantages, hurts and adverse circumstances belong to millions of people. You can

light a candle; you have knowledge to guide people out of the chains that bind them; to help them."

She gave me ten reasons, including, "You'll have a special item for your coffee table," showing Linda knows the treasure of play, one of our Happiness Action Tools™.

We All Deserve to Be Happy

We all deserve to be happy, feel self-confident and feel equipped to handle life. We all deserve to respect ourselves enough to stand up for what is rightfully ours, which includes being happy. Remember a time when you felt on top of the world, a time when you felt you could conquer anything, a time when you felt powerful and joyful. What would your life be like if you could feel that powerful most of the time? Now you can.

Rich or poor a child can experience the cruelties, or just inadvertent neglect, that spurs darkness that grows and covers that spark of confidence that could be a flame to their finding their purpose and maybe opening the doors wide to that sense of well-being known as happiness. My hope is that you will find a flame that does spark that confidence to finding your purpose opening wide your sense of well-being.

You will find happiness techniques herein you can use. It may take repetition to get the best results, however achieving this reward is within the grasp of anyone. You, too, can live a more peaceful existence and more often approach life with joyful anticipation – instead of fearful trepidation or, even worse, resignation. You really can be happy most of the time.

I practice what I preach. I use these Happiness Action Tools™. I don't use all of them at once or all the time. Yet, when I feel emotionally low, my friends remind me to read my own book! Fortunately, most have become good habits.

Trosein, aka The Cosmic Waverider, is my brother, David's cartoon character who rides light waves, sound waves and happiness waves along with real waves. He said, "The Happiness Book is not just another laugh – it has ways on how to ride the wave of happiness for the rest of time."

I feel so blessed, more because of the peace I feel within myself than because of material things in my life. I still have times when I feel hurt, disappointment, anger, or other less noble human emotions. My ability to refocus myself with positive thoughts and actions just comes easier and more spontaneously now.

Now I know I am worthy and can have what I want in life. What seem to be miracles now appear regularly in my life. I truly am living in joyful anticipation. You see, I do have the right to tell you that you can transform your life to a happier one – because I discovered how. **I do have the right to tell you that you can LEARN to be happy, because I did!**

Edwin Markham expressed, "There is a destiny which makes us brothers; none goes his way alone. All that we send into the lives of others comes back into our own."

If I can share just one thing that will add to someone's much needed self-esteem, or direct one wandering soul to its purpose, or open up someone's thinking to let happiness in, I will have served a great purpose. And, isn't that a happy thought? ☺

I believe, as Anne Frank did, that "Everyone has inside of him a piece of good news. The good news is that you don't know how great you can be! How much you can love! What you can accomplish! And what your potential is!" Everyone has the potential to be happy and I know we can all achieve it.

What I have to share can help transform you into a beautiful butterfly and help make the lives of your friends happier – and their friends happier – and their friends happier, and...

My hope is you will find peace, purpose and greater happiness. I am living proof that we can overcome the injustices that life throws at us. I see myself as having transformed into that butterfly we can all be, flying free and happy.

CHAPTER ONE

What is Happiness Really?

THE ULTIMATE ANTI-AGING SOLUTION

*"Happiness is the meaning and the purpose of life,
the whole aim and end of human existence."*
~ Aristotle

*"Happiness is a journey, not a destination;
happiness is to be found along the way
not at the end of the road,
for then the journey is over and it's too late.
The time for happiness is today not tomorrow."*
~ Joseph Smith Jr.

*"To seek happiness outside of ourselves
is like trying to lasso a cloud.
Happiness is not a thing; it is a state of mind."*
~ Omar Khayyam

So, what is happiness really? And, why isn't everyone happy? These certainly are questions worth pondering. In *THE ART OF HAPPINESS*, the Dalai Lama and Howard C. Cutler, M.D., proposed that the purpose of our existence is to seek happiness. They say, "Western thinkers from Aristotle to William James have agreed with this idea."

The *DAILY GURU* expressed, "What, then, is happiness? The answer is not complex. Happiness is simply a state of inner freedom. Freedom from what? With a bit of self-insight, every individual can answer that question for himself. It is freedom from the secret angers and anxieties we tell no one about. It is freedom from fear of being unappreciated and ignored, from muddled thinking that drives us to compulsive actions, and later, to regrets. It is freedom from painful cravings that deceive us into thinking that our attainment of this person or of that circumstance will make everything right."

It is a pleasure to be happy. Yet, pleasure is not the same thing as happiness. Pleasure is temporary and usually based on an outside circumstance. Happiness, on the other hand, is a state of mind. *WEBSTER DICTIONARY* defines it as "a state of well being characterized by emotions ranging from contentment to intense joy." According to Mahatma Gandhi, "Happiness is when what you think, what you say, and what you do are in harmony."

I define happiness as being without fear; having that sense of well being that comes from being so at ease with who you are that you are excited about how you are living your life. This is not about the kind of happiness that shows up for one manic moment then quickly disappears. Nor is it everlasting giddiness, although you may have more of that than you do now. It is an underlying sense of peace, confidence, contentment and an appreciation of life, the way it is in this moment and the way it can be in the future. It is the ultimate anti-aging solution!

Being Happy is Being Successful

I really believe that if you are happy you are successful. Note that I said you are successful when you are happy; **not** you are happy when you are successful. Albert Sweitzer agreed with me, "Success is not the key to happiness. Happiness is the key to success. If you love what you are doing, you will be successful."

Happiness is different for each of us. What makes one happy might not make another happy. That is the interesting tapestry of life – our unique overlapping individualities. You may find your journey to happiness takes you places you might not have considered.

Be open to new ideas on how you can reach your desired destination. Don't be your "own worst enemy" by letting your preconceived notion or expectation of perfection get in the way. If you find the path you've chosen takes you in a direction that doesn't fully support you, know that, while in route, you have the freedom to make adjustments and changes. Getting to the peak of the mountain may require detours; however, the destination remains the same. We may even find more happiness along this route. ☺

Norman Lear shared, "Success is how you collect your minutes. You spend millions of minutes to reach one triumph, one moment. Then you spend maybe a thousand minutes enjoying it. If you were unhappy through those millions of minutes, what good is the thousand minutes of triumph?"

He went on, "It doesn't equate. How many successful people end up suicides? Life is made of small pleasures, good eye contact over the breakfast table with your wife, a moment of touching a friend. Happiness is made of the tiny successes. The big ones come infrequently. If you don't love all of those zillion of tiny successes, the big ones don't mean anything. If there's one thing I want my children to learn from me it is to take pleasure in life's daily successes. It's the most important thing I've learned."

Having Money Doesn't Make Us Happy

Many people think money will make them happy. Most of us know someone who has more money than he or she can ever spend, and, yet, is not happy.

Ask yourself which you would prefer: To have a lot of money and power and yet not be happy, or have very little or no money and yet be truly happy? Research supports the fact that additional income (over and above a level of survival) does little to raise our sense of satisfaction with life.

It is what we do with money that counts toward our happiness. Keith DeGreen said, "To the extent that money is a measure of the services we perform for others, its accumulation is noble. To the extent that we press our money into the services of those we love to provide them with as warm and as secure an existence as possible, its disbursement is inspired and divine."

Having money, a nice house or a fancy car may be outward manifestations that reflect the outcome of our actions. Yet, we are worthy without any of those things.

Mother Teresa was not a wealthy woman and she certainly did not care what kind of car she rode in. Still she is one of the most revered women of all time.

William Barclay pointed out, "Joy has nothing to do with material things, or with man's outward circumstance. A man living in the lap of luxury can be wretched, and a man in the depths of poverty can overflow with joy."

True Life Example: My friend, Dr. Anthony Gergely, shared a story that applies to this discussion about money and happiness:

> "Being one of thirteen children has often caused me to wonder how my parents were able to make it impossible for me to ever think that we were poor. We had food, shelter, clothing, and love. We had everything: although my dad never made more than $60 dollars a week making train wheels in the steel mill. Yes, I dreamt of all kinds of toys: especially, an electric freight train, which never arrived at my 'station' under our annual live Scottish Irish Christmas tree. Years later, many years later, in an antique shop, covered with a coating of children's love and dust, sat a train, freight cars and all. For twenty years now, that train has gone round and round under our annual live Scottish Irish Christmas tree and I can recall a beautiful little girl looking puzzling at me one Christmas morning and saying – 'Dad, I can't figure out if we are rich or poor.' And I asked, 'Are you asking about money or happiness?' She thought for a moment and then started playing with the train."

Seeking Happiness is Not Self-Centered

Many of us would question whether seeking personal happiness isn't self-centered, maybe even self-indulgent. Happiness research repeatedly shows **unhappy** people are actually the most self-absorbed.

In the book *THE ART OF HAPPINESS* by The Dalai Lama and Dr. Cutler it was written, "Happy people, in contrast, are generally found to be more sociable, flexible, and creative and are able to tolerate life's daily frustrations more easily than unhappy people. And, most important, they are found to be more loving and forgiving than unhappy people."

Loving ourselves is not selfish. **We simply <u>must</u> care for ourselves first; we can't give what isn't there!** If we sacrifice ourselves because we feel unworthy, we blindly abandon life. If we give ourselves away then what is left? Nothing! There is nothing for us to give to anyone, not even ourselves. My brother, David Stearns, said it beautifully, "Self-esteem is saving a place in our hearts for our self."

Dr. Norman Vincent Peale said, "Believe in yourself! Have faith in your abilities! Without a humble but reasonable confidence in your own powers you cannot be successful or happy."

Loving ourselves, we have love overflowing and the strength to follow our feelings through with positive actions. We are no longer self-absorbed or needing to focus on our needs or obsessions. We have no guilt in wanting the best for ourselves for we know we are capable of more abundant giving.

Happiness is a Mindset

Prosperity for the purposes of this book is "being happy." You see, I believe prosperity and happiness are mindsets. I believe prosperity is a state of consciousness not necessarily reflected in our outer material world. Are we not the wealthiest when we are the happiest?

It is interesting to note that the word "wealth" comes from the Anglo Saxon 13th century word "weal" defined as "well-being, prosperity, or happiness." The Middle English word was welth modeled on health, again related to happiness and well-being. The association of the word to monetary riches seems to have come about in the 15th century.

So prosperity is happiness; it's a state of consciousness and not a reflection of what we have in material possessions. We are the wealthiest and the happiest when we are consciously feeling a sense of well being, which is most often not about money or material possessions.

Have you ever noticed that some of the poorest people are the happiest? The people of India are truly some of the poorest people in the world, yet there is a book entitled *CITY OF HOPE*, which is a testament to their happiness.

It's also true that some of the richest people are the unhappiest. "One man's trash is another man's treasure," so the expression goes. It's a matter of attitude. How much is enough and how much of what? There's a wish passed down from generation to generation that talks about *enough*. I think it answers my question beautifully. Here it is:

> *I wish you enough sun to keep your attitude bright.*
> *I wish you enough rain to appreciate the sun more.*
> *I wish you enough happiness to keep your spirit alive.*
> *I wish you enough pain so that the smallest joys in life appear bigger.*
> *I wish you enough gain to satisfy your wanting.*
> *I wish you enough loss to appreciate all that you possess.*
> *I wish you enough hellos to get you through the final goodbye.*

Genneine Bondy inspired us with, "Your life is a gift, unwrap it with joy." Focus on really caring for yourself. Allow a sense of self worth by nurturing yourself to increase your happiness. Remember, you can learn to be happy.

Fydor Dostoevsky said, "To love a man is to see him as God intended him to be." So, love yourself so you can become what God intends you to be! (Which I believe is "happy!")

What Does Make Us Happier?

The big question is, "What does make us happier?" Actually just acting happier makes us happier, among other things.

Interestingly, appreciating the little things in our life, not the big events, brings us greater joy and happiness. Peter Thomson said, "In a world where the big things have little difference – it's the little things that make a big difference."

We can significantly increase our happiness levels through simple changes in lifestyle and cognitive behavioral changes. This means developing new habits and new ways of doing things, both in our physical and our mental worlds. You now have the Happiness Action Tools™ in your hand to assist you in achieving your happiest life.

The Pie Chart for Happiness

Sonja Lyubomirsky, Research Psychologist and University of California Professor of Psychology has a pie chart in her book, *THE HOW OF HAPPINESS*, which shows what she, and fellow Professors, Ken Sheldon and David Schkade have concluded determines happiness. According to the chart, we are born with a "set point" or disposition that makes up 50 percent of the chart. The chart also shows that another 10 percent of our happiness is determined by circumstances.

So, yes, winning the lottery, getting an award or a gift or having a successful relationship can bring about an increase in happiness, however small or temporary it may be. What is astounding, according to this chart, is that **40 percent of what determines our happiness is a "choice" and therefore, within our power to change!**

A Decade Longer!

Most of us, if we're honest, don't very much like the idea of aging. Yet, studies have shown that we get happier as we age. Age doesn't have to be an enemy.

Although there is no way to stop the clock, you can take good care of yourself to forestall the physical signs of aging. Just as importantly, you can keep your attitude in tune. Age is just a number that says how long you've been living in your physical body. You can always have a hand in the conscientious care of that body, just as you can do things to keep your mind alert and your emotions healthy.

Studies show that happiness brings us physical, mental and emotional health. Our emotional health brings more cooperation, sociability and charitableness along with greater self-control and coping abilities. We are likely to have more friends and a stronger support system.

Our optimism affects our health and life span, as well as our sense of well-being. Studies reveal that if we are happy we will have a stronger immune system, more energy and **a longer life, one that could be as much as a decade longer!**

Other benefits of happiness include a happier work life, which could be attributable to clarity of mind, increased productivity, and greater creativity all brought on by being happy.

With all our advancements in technology and health there are many people who do not look or act their age. Yet much of the time, it's the happy people who look the youngest – must be something about the glow. After all, a smile is the most attractive thing we can wear!

Butterflies never show their age. Happiness truly is the ultimate anti-aging solution!

CHAPTER TWO

Action is the Key

The Force of Taking Action

"What you can do or dream you can, begin it; boldness has genius, power and magic in it."
~ Johann Wolfgang von Goethe

"We judge ourselves by what we feel capable of doing, while others judge us by what we have already done."
~ Henry Wadsworth Longfellow

"Action may not always bring happiness; but there is no happiness without action."
~ Benjamin Disraeli

This chapter begins with my favorite quote. To me the message of this quote is **"take action."** It might have read, "What you can do, or dream you can, **take action**..."

Happy people are action oriented knowing that taking action is the key to getting what they want in life. Jack Canfield expressed, "Everything you want is out there waiting for you to ask. Everything you want also wants you. But you have to take action to get it." Dr. Robert Anthony, one of my very favorite authors, said, "It is not enough to know what to do, you must do what you know."

Action is the key to change. **I am convinced that action is the most significant thing you can do to empower yourself.** Action is truly the catalyst. You can learn about, talk about, philosophize about, and desire to change things. However, **without action, nothing happens, ABSOLUTELY NOTHING.** Joe Sabah shared that, "You do not have to be great to start, but you have to start to be great." An unknown author said, "One of the most amazing miracles ever is being prepared when the opportunity presents itself."

ACTION IS THE KEY

If you know what it is you want to accomplish, then start moving toward it. This doesn't mean you leave home with nothing but your toothbrush and guitar. It does mean beginning to do the things that put you in the right direction. That might mean getting more education or joining groups that lead you there. Just take action.

Dorothy Corkville Briggs in her book *CELEBRATE YOUR SELF* said, "Awareness, courage and decision need to be coupled with action. Recipes in books don't bake cookies. You do – through action. Blueprints on paper don't build bridges. People hard at work do. Here are the tools you need. But only you can decide to use them, to practice them daily." As Maya Angelou put it, "Nothing will work unless you do."

You have the Happiness Action Tools™ to live your happiest life right here. However, **only you can put them into practice.** Nolan Bushnell expressed, "Everyone who has ever taken a shower has had an idea. It's the person who gets out of the shower, dries off, and does something about it that makes a difference."

Action is the Catalyst

Action is such a positive thing. Action is movement and motion. Action energizes and mobilizes us; it moves us forward. Action is healthy physically as well as emotionally as it creates positive chemicals, called endorphins, in our bodies.

Dr. Norman Vincent Peale said, "Action is the restorer and builder of confidence. Inaction is not only the result, but the cause of fear. Perhaps the action you take will be successful; perhaps different action or adjustments will have to follow. But any action is better than no action at all."

Making the conscious decision to take action we turn the tide of life in our favor. Action has a way of increasing opportunity in most unusual ways leading us to new and interesting endeavors. Every time you put off decisive action, you are delaying getting the prize.

The dictionary defines "power" as, "the ability to do or act." Therefore, in essence, this book is about power because it is about action; empowering Happiness Action Tools™ we can act on to live our best and, therefore, happiest life.

This is not another book expounding philosophies; it shares 21 tools, complete with how-to; actions anyone can utilize to experience more happiness and fuel your best life with direction, speed and energy. Happiness will give you energy – energy to take action. The easy to do Actions herein will improve your life if you put them in force regularly.

Action cures fear. It's all about action. **Life is really quite simple – if something in our life doesn't work – change it, move away from it or accept it!** I call this the "THEORY OF THREE." If you can't accept something, take the action of changing it. If you can't change it, choose to move away from it! If you choose to stay, you still have the power of knowing it was your choice to accept it.

The best way to escape a problem is to solve it. My friend (and writing partner), Linda Hancock Moore said, "A problem does not present itself without an answer somewhere in it." The famed Dottie Walters believed, "The solution is always at hand." Lee Iacocca expressed, "Apply yourself. Get all the education you can, but then, by God, do something. Don't just stand there, make it happen."

True Life Example: Margot Fonteyn, the legendary ballerina, when asked how she survived her many challenges in life, answered, "I have no idea. I was performing; I simply got out there and danced. And I live that way too. I don't analyze. I just get on with it." That's what my friend Alice, did. She didn't analyze, she just got on with it. She taught me if you go ahead and do something, before you know it, the task is finished.

A Look at the Words "Hope" and "Try"

We often use the words "hope" and "try." I **hope** I will. I **hope** I can. We may limit ourselves when we use those words. Deciding not to take action (out of fear) is like making an excuse in advance. Having **tried**, we use that as an excuse to give up, and **hoping** takes the place of any real effort on our part.

We don't want to stop trying or give up hope. Let's just put them into proper perspective. I recognize the positive interpretations of these words. **Try** is the first step after the decision to do and **hope** is a messenger that the dreams we have are signs of our unlimited possibilities.

Trying is for different foods our mother encourages us to eat to expand our tastes and keep us from wasting food. **Hope** is a friend to all, especially to the Action of courage. As we are about to jump into that unknown (where all those imaginary monsters dwell), **hope** stands beside us, and reminds us that there, too, resides all our potential good. However, look at the word **try** from another perspective. Drop a pen on the floor, and then lean down and try to pick it up. Either you pick it up or you don't pick it up. You really can't try to do it. You really can't **try** to do anything. **Trying can be a smoke screen for the inability to commit, setting us up for disappointment**.

Just think before you use the words hope or try. Those words may imply possible failure. The statements, "I will", "I intend" or "I plan" show probable accomplishment. David Copperfield said, "The most important thing in life is to **stop saying, 'I wish' and start saying 'I will'**." *[Emphasis added.]*

Check your intentions for substance and clarity. Your intentions are your motivations, your heat seeking missiles. If based in integrity and full of heart, you need to be clear as to the target, and then just do it.

Dr. Robert Anthony said, "**Excuses are lack of faith in our own power**. If we simply wish and hope for something to happen, we are not utilizing the force of action." As James Russell Lowell said, "All the sentiments in the world weigh less than one lovely action!" *[Emphasis added.]*

Warning! Think Before You Leap

As important as taking action is, think before you leap. Don't be busy just to be busy! Spend your energy on productive action.

The power of the thought behind the action is sometimes more significant than the action itself, especially when we recognize that thinking is also an action. Thought is what manifests in your outside world.

However, there is a balance between thinking and doing. **Don't be so caught up in thinking that you never take action. Definitely don't be preoccupied with mindless doing or you will end up with mindless results.** Come from intelligent intention and thought, then act.

This is even better if you add passion to the mix, but above all, come from the balance of the two; thought and action. Hitting the mark one has inspired to, with passion, often explodes into a multitude of wonderful results you never consciously imagined.

One Step at a Time

We take action one-step at a time. In his book, *THE MAGIC OF THINKING BIG*, David J. Swartz said it well: "The person determined to achieve maximum success learns the principle that progress is made one step at a time. A house is built a brick at a time. Football games are won a play at a time. A department store grows bigger one new customer at a time. **Big accomplishments are a series of little accomplishments.**" *[Emphasis added.]*

Many people have commented on this. Lao Tzu said, "The journey of a thousand miles begins with a single step." Henry David Thoreau said, "There is no beginning too small." Al Bernstein shared, "Sometimes the fool who rushes in gets the job done."

If you don't start, it's certain you won't finish. William Blake told us, "Execution is the chariot of genius." Will Rogers said, "Even if you are on the right track, you'll get run over if you just sit there."

As my favorite quote that starts this chapter says, **"Whatever you dream you can do... just begin it."** Experts agree we can accomplish big goals by breaking them into smaller doable daily actions. Mark Twain expressed, "The secret of getting ahead is getting started.

The secret of getting started is breaking your complex overwhelming tasks into small manageable tasks, and then starting on the first one."A house is built one board or one brick at a time. Even a few a boards a day will get that house built. Remember the advertisements Nike had with the slogan "*JUST DO IT!*" What a powerful statement!

True Life Example: An employment counselor didn't really enjoy her job. Unfortunately, she needed her paycheck. She could have just moaned and complained, which is what many do – nothing really.

However, she decided to take action. She investigated what she did not like; for instance, was it the people she was working with? If so, she could have just decided to get another job as an employment counselor. Yet she liked the people she worked with very much. She realized she didn't get any sense of real accomplishment (except for paying her bills). She did get a sense of contribution by helping people find appropriate jobs. However, her position was very stressful mentally leaving her drained at night, so she did not pursue her creative activities, which were very important to her.

She needed to find a way to earn a living that would offer her a sense of accomplishment, a sense of contribution, contact with people, *and* a way to pay her bills, all in less hours so she could have time to pursue her creative projects.

Her solution was to get a job as a flight attendant. She cared for the passengers and she was able to have stress-free time to pursue her creative activities. Experiencing the world in a way often only experienced by the wealthy was another benefit. She was rewarded in ways she never would have imagined by taking the action of changing circumstances she didn't like.

Next time she may decide on a job that more specifically allows her to express her creativity. In the meantime she enhanced her life by imagining her life different, better, taking the responsibility to make the changes necessary, and believing those possibilities into fruition. No matter what the circumstances are, **if you take action you facilitate movement and change.**

Slay the Demon of Delay

We are all guilty of procrastination at one time or another. We then waste even more time criticizing ourselves for procrastinating!

We may procrastinate to avoid something or because we have a need for perfection. Instead of just doing something to the best of our ability now, we put it off until we have more information on how to do it right, have better tools, or someone can help us with it. Often if we just go ahead and do whatever it is with what is at hand, it turns out better than we expected or even imagined.

Is what you are avoiding worth the energy you are putting into avoiding it? What will happen if you don't do this now? Maybe it really isn't that important, and you can *choose* to let it go.

If you decide it is necessary then just do it and get on with your life. Now you can put that precious energy into positive action with the BIG payoff: feeling good about yourself. You will also get that great sense of relief!

A simple idea for overcoming procrastination from time management experts is to commit to making an effort toward a project for only ten or twenty minutes. When your time is up you probably will be motivated enough to continue.

Barbara Sher said, "'Now' is the operative word. Everything you put in your way is just a method of putting off the hour when you could actually be living your dream. You don't need endless time and perfect conditions. Do it now. Do it today. Do it for twenty minutes and watch your heart start beating."

Starting with a small action, we can often accomplish major feats. It can be just a small action. The action of beginning something makes the whole project feel achievable.

Action is in the NOW, in the PRESENT. My mother said it profoundly, **"We are all so busy becoming, when all we need to do is be."** An unknown author put it this way, "remember yesterday, dream about tomorrow — but live today!"

ACTION IS THE KEY

There's the expression, "After all is said and done, much is said and little is done." If you don't start, it's certain you won't arrive. So, go take action to live your happiest life!

Positive Expectation Statement™

For Taking Action

"I enjoy taking effective positive action!"

(6 words)

For free gifts to support you in being your happiest, visit your happiness community at TheHappinessCommunity.com.

PART 2

The Tools with Instructions for Use

CHAPTER THREE

Be a Sailboat with a Keel

HAPPINESS ACTION TOOL™ #1
THE EFFECTIVENESS OF DECISIVENESS

"Once you make a decision,
the universe conspires to make it happen."
~ Ralph Waldo Emerson

"Analysis of over twenty-five thousand men and woman who had experienced failure disclosed the fact that lack of decision was near the head of the list of the thirty-one major causes of failure."
~ Napoleon Hill

"The block of granite which was an obstacle
in the pathway of the weak
becomes a stepping-stone in the pathway of the strong.
That block of granite is often nothing more than a decision."
~ Thomas Carlyle

Decide now to have a happier life. Making a decision is crucial to everything as it is the first action before we do anything else. The simple act of making a decision is very powerful as very few actions come without a corresponding decision to do so.

The definition of a decision is "the act of making up one's mind." Therefore, in order to have a better life we have to make up our mind to do so. We first have to decide to have a better life.

An unknown author pointed out that, "One good wish changes nothing. One good decision changes everything." David Mahoney put it like this, "Some people say a decision has to marinate before you can make it. Sometimes that is true. However, you will never have all the information you need to make a decision. If you did, it would be a foregone conclusion, not a decision." Ben Stein stated, "The indispensable first step to getting the things you want out of life is this: decide what you want."

Making a decision can change your life. As Dr. Robert H. Schuller expressed, "Again and again, **the impossible problem is solved when we see that the problem is only a tough decision waiting to be made."**

Nothing Happens Without a Decision

Almost nothing happens without a decision first. Our breathing and blood flow, of course, are exceptions, and even those are known to change with deep concentration. So it's safe to say decision predicates almost every other action we might take.

Indecision is one of the major causes of failure. Right or wrong, a decision comes before an action. If we make a wrong decision, we can make another one to repair or replace the first decision.

As Harry Truman told us, "A man who's willing to make a decision in the first place, can always make another one to correct any mistake he's made." If we make no decision, we are still making a decision: we are making the decision of no action. And, what happens with no action? Nothing! Neil Peart said it well, **"If you choose not to decide, you still have made a choice."**

Act As If

True Life Example: While attending UPWARD BOUND at 17, in addition to cultural events and learning, I had a mind expansion. I realized since the other students did not know me I could "act" confident and they might not know that I was actually insecure.

I learned a valuable lesson that summer; that others perceive us, as we appear to be. "Act as if" and that is how others will see you. I was "Ms. Insecure Wallflower" at my high school and here I was "Ms. Confident Popularity."

I first decided. I decided to act as if I had self-esteem and in doing so, *gained* a tremendous amount of self-esteem, which began building my happiness. I learned from my experiment that summer. I continued learning by observing other people, extensive reading, and training from classes and seminars, learning the tools I now use every day. With these new thoughts and habits, I am more receptive to happiness.

A Decision is a Conscious Choice

A decision is a conscious choice. Just deciding you want to do something is half the battle. Remember that every choice comes with consequences. So, be conscious and choose wisely, however still, make a decision.

When you are in emotional pain, you can let the hurt shape you into a stronger, happier person or you can feel victimized, perpetuating a destructive holding pattern for yourself. You make the decision either way. Ask yourself what the benefits or the repercussions are of making this decision.

You may not always be able to control what happens to you. However, you are always in charge of how you respond, as in "responsibility" which is defined as the ability to respond.

Bill Burns shared that, "We can block ourselves and cut ourselves out of life by such negative reactions as anger, fear, jealousy, self-pity or resentment. Instead, let's give up these emotional traps and convert our energies to hope, excitement, commitment, motivation and fulfillment." You can decide to think positively and be happy.

Indecision is a Major Cause of Failure

Napoleon Hill in THINK AND GROW RICH stated that, "Analysis of over twenty-five thousand men and women who had experienced failure disclosed the fact that **lack of decision was near the head of the list of the thirty-one major causes of failure**. Procrastination, the opposite of decision, is a common enemy, which practically every person must conquer." *[Emphasis added.]*

Procrastination is the most common way of avoiding any task, including that of making a decision. **Procrastination, combined with indecision, can take more time and energy than to make a decision in the first place.** Then there is the stress of all that indecision and procrastination, adding to the complexity of whatever the fear one might have had in making the decision in the first place. You would think we would want to make a decision just for the relief.

After analyzing hundreds of people who had accumulated great fortunes, Hill found that **every single one of them** had the habit of reaching decisions promptly. Moreover, once they had made their decisions, they were very slow in changing their minds. In contrast, Hill concluded, **"People who fail to accumulate money, without exception, have the habit of reaching decisions very slowly, if at all, and of changing these decisions, quickly and often."** *[Emphasis added.]*

Hill also said that, "opinions are the cheapest commodities on earth... that many unsuccessful people are easily influenced by the opinions of others and... if you are influenced by the opinions of others, you will have no desire of your own."

Make a Decision and Stick to It

Having made a decision it is important to stand by it. Certainly leave room for adjustments, yet do not vacillate. We can end up in a state of frustration if we are swayed by every opinion. This wastes more valuable time and energy. With each successful decision, we will have greater confidence in the powerful attribute of decisiveness.

Certainly obtain wise counsel. Some choices are easy while others require more profound analysis and deep soul searching. If you trust yourself, you more easily make decisions. You can re-think any particulars of your decision, if necessary – the question to ask is if this is just your own self-sabotage at work.

All of us know people who cannot stick to a decision. They go through life like a sailboat without a keel, tipping at the slightest gusts. They reach their goals only with the greatest amount of trouble, sometimes maybe never reaching them at all. Eventually this can lead to emotional imbalance and mental instability.

William James said, "There is no more miserable human being than one in whom nothing is habitual but indecision." Decisiveness is essential for a healthy, productive life. Making a decision can change your life. However not making a decision can also change our life. Procrastinate and you are doomed to failure. Let's face it: indecision and procrastination don't get results and hold no rewards. Start an action with a firm decision – and the intention of sticking to it.

How to Be Decisive

1. **Clear your head.** You need a clear head to analyze your choices wisely. Step away by doing something else for a while allowing your subconscious to work on it.
2. **Write down all your options.** Write down your thoughts and organize them into pros and cons, to give you clarity. Give a weight to each pro and con and run a total on each. Do they balance (or not)?
3. **Sleep on it.** This gives your higher consciousness a chance to contribute to the decision you need to reach. As you go to sleep, tell yourself that you will awake with clarity as to the right action to take.

We waste so much energy on procrastination and worry. Stephen Lau in his newsletter, *LONGETIVITY FOR YOU*, wrote, "Worrying about the future will cause distress in the present; despairing about the past will cripple you in the present. So, live in the eternal now, and you will have power over both the past and the future. Always live in the present."

Live in the present by deciding things quickly yet with forethought, all the while trusting your intuition. This will put you one-step closer to happiness. Anne O'Hare McCormick, shared, "The percentage of mistakes in quick decisions is no greater than in long-drawn-out vacillation, and the effect of decisiveness itself 'makes things go' and creates confidence."

It is my belief that our first decision, especially if intuitive, is the right one. Yes, I definitely believe in trusting my higher self for decision-making. Often our intuitive thoughts are more important than the thoughts rolling around in our head.

That is why I say, "sleep on it" after turning it over to your higher self. This allows time for your mind chatter to quiet down. Get the facts first and then just trust knowing that you will make the right decision. Sometimes we are so busy trying to figure it out that we don't allow the answer to come in!

BE A SAILBOAT WITH A KEEL

Abraham Lincoln said, "Determine that a thing can and shall be done, and then we shall find the way." The quote from Ralph Waldo Emerson that started this chapter summed it up beautifully, "Once you make a decision, the universe conspires to make it happen."

Another important point is to remember this is *your* decision. It's okay to seek advice, however still sleep on it. This decision is about what is best for you and your happiness. Just stay in integrity by considering the outcome for everyone involved.

Still, sometimes we make other people's welfare more important than our own by worrying about how our choices will affect them. Ironically, what we think may be the best for others they would not even agree is the best for them.

Besides, when making our best choices out of integrity, we end up doing what is best for others, too. So, ponder thoughtfully, and then sleep on it.

Once you have made your decision, be happy with it. Don't second-guess it! Decide to live your happiest life! **Make the decision today to get happy and stay happy!**

Positive Expectation Statement™

For Happiness Action Tool™ #1
THE EFFECTIVENESS OF DECISIVENESS

"I now make effective decisions easily."

(6 words)

For free gifts to support you in being your happiest, visit your happiness community at TheHappinessCommunity.com.

CHAPTER FOUR

Take a Chance and Be Great

HAPPINESS ACTION TOOL™ #2
THE ENERGY OF COURAGE

"Courage is the greatest of all the virtues.
Because if you haven't courage,
you may not have an opportunity to use any of the others."
~ Samuel Johnson

"Twenty years from now you will be more disappointed
by the things that you didn't do than by the ones you did do.
So throw off the bowlines.
Sail away from the safe harbor.
Catch the trade winds in your sails.
Explore. Dream. Discover."
~ Mark Twain

"Our doubts are traitors, and make us lose the good
we oft might win - by fearing to attempt."
~ William Shakespeare

Courage is significant to self-esteem and happiness. Taking action can be risky and can involve courage; yet taking action is critical to achieving anything in life. As T.S. Elliot put it, **"Only those who risk going too far can possibly find out how far they can go."**

Malcolm Forbes said, "Venture nothing, and life is less than it should be." Jimmy Johnson asked, "Do you want to be safe and good, or do you want to take a chance and be great?"

If you want your life to be different, you have to change and change requires courage. View these Happiness Action Tools™ as growth-enhancing and empowering adventures. Approach them with joyful anticipation. You really can have fun with them.

TAKE A CHANCE AND BE GREAT

My friend, Lenny Johnson, shared this from Ashley Brilliant, "Haven't we always known that change is the one constant that we have had to deal with on a daily basis? As for myself, I love the element of change. It spices up what sometimes would be extremely dull and boring day-to-day living."

The most difficult thing about change is making the decision to change. It takes courage to set things in motion.

Theodore Roosevelt stated, "Far better to dare mighty things, to win glorious triumphs, even though checkered by failure, than to take rank with those poor spirits who neither enjoy much nor suffer much, because they live in the gray twilight that knows not victory, nor defeat."

Robert F. Kennedy proclaimed, "It is from numberless diverse acts of courage and belief that human history is shaped. Each time a man stands up for an ideal, or acts to improve the lot of others, or strikes out against injustice, he sends forth a tiny ripple of hope, and crossing each other from a million different centers of energy and daring those ripples build a current which can sweep down the mightiest walls of oppression and injustice."

Courage is an Action

Did you know that courage is not a feeling? It is an action. It is something that we do to overcome the fear of unfamiliar or frightening situations. "Courage is not the absence of fear but the ability to carry on with dignity in spite of it," said Scott Turow.

The wise Eleanor Roosevelt said, "You gain strength, courage, and confidence by every experience in which you really stop to look fear in the face. You must do the thing which you think you cannot do."

Confronting our fears and tackling challenges may mean we need to take a risk. It takes courage to face an emotional challenge or accomplish an overwhelming set of tasks. For people with physical disabilities sometimes just the simple act of getting out of bed takes tremendous courage.

TAKE A CHANCE AND BE GREAT

Every act of courage changes the world. Perhaps not in a major way, yet your life would certainly be different if you didn't get out of that bed, wouldn't it?

Taking risks means pushing our comfort zone to new limits. By being willing to expand our comfort zones, we allow ourselves to experience life more fully. Andre Gide said, "Man cannot discover new oceans unless he has the courage to lose sight of the shore."

True Life Example: There was a woman who couldn't swim. She had been horribly afraid of deep water all her life, yet her dream of being a flight attendant was even greater.

When confronted with the hardest swim test anyone could have asked her to perform, she amazed herself by taking a deep breath and jumping in. The teacher's response was, "You have the kind of courage they are looking for." The woman thought to herself, "There is a God. He does walk on water, and He took my swim test for me." Truth is she had been willing to "lose sight of the shore," and discovered her greater potential existed well beyond her restrictive comfort zone.

Challenge the Fear

Our fears show up because of our subconscious resistance to change, which comes from a survival level. Let's challenge the fear to allow for a richer, happier life.

Anne Morrow Lindbergh expressed that, "We tend not to choose the unknown, which might be a shock or a disappointment or simply a little difficult to cope with. And yet, **it is the unknown with all of its disappointments and surprises that is the most enriching."**

Jim Rohn said, "Fears, even the most basic ones, can totally destroy our ambitions. Fear can destroy fortunes. Fear can destroy relationships. Fear, if left unchecked, can destroy our lives. Fear is one of the many enemies lurking inside us."

Jack Canfield shared, "Almost everything we'll ever do in life that is really powerful, that really produces a result in our lives, that quantum-leaps us to a new level... requires us to do something uncomfortable. It takes risks to achieve. It's often scary. It requires something you didn't know before or a skill you didn't have before. But in the end, it's worth it."

As former Congressman Ed Forman put it, "Winners are those people who make a habit of doing things losers are uncomfortable doing. Make today your day to start that uncomfortable new habit."

Again, I quote Dr. Robert Anthony, **"The greatest risk is not taking a risk."** Hear ye! Hear ye! "Many things are lost for want of asking," according to an English proverb.

I'm not talking about risks like rock climbing, skydiving, walking across hot coals, or being shot from a canon, although if you feel inspired to climb a mountain you must answer the call as your head and heart dictate. A wise concern for safety is fundamental to all human beings.

As well, you need to take a risk now and then in order to reach your full potential. I am suggesting that as Helen Keller shared, "Security does not exist in nature, nor do the children of men as a whole experience it. Avoiding danger is no safer in the long run than exposure. Life is either a daring adventure or nothing."

For our purposes, let's consider taking risks as meaning daring to try new approaches or ideas with no predictable control over results or consequences, i.e., taking action when the outcome is unknown. And, the way you can take those risks is with courage. Dwight D. Eisenhower said of courage, "What counts is not necessarily the size of the dog in the fight, but the size of the fight in the dog."

Courage is Taking Action in Spite of Fear

Fear is the greatest obstacle to our happiness. The dictionary defines fear as the "apprehension of impending danger" or the "anticipation of pain." The definition of "anticipation" is "something expected." Therefore, if anticipation is expected, it is not in the present; it is in the future. **It is only something we have imagined and does not really exist**. With that idea clear, act courageously against fear: it's an imaginary foe. The same reality applies to the fear of making a mistake. It is something we anticipate. It is in the future. We are imagining it. In fact, we might just do it correctly!

Fear can have no power over us unless we give it that power. Our mind, however, goes back and retrieves events that did not have a successful outcome. In the effort to protect us, our minds manufacture fear. It figures that if we don't try anything new we will be safe. One of its favorite expressions is, "What if?" attached to a number of possible outcomes.

The reality is the chance of any of these things happening is very unlikely. Recognize that it isn't always good to believe your protective mind, realizing that its purpose is to protect you. You don't have to listen to it. Act in spite of the fear. Say to your mind, "Thank you for sharing," and take action anyway.

One of my favorite "Words to Live By" (Appendix A) is, "What is the worst thing that might happen? And what is the worst thing about that?" Sometimes I ask the question repeatedly to a point of ridiculousness – which is actually the point!

Mark Victor Hansen has a great answer: "Most of the time we'll find out that the 'thing' was not that scary after all. Our imaginations had behaved like a super fertilizer and grown a grotesque monstrosity in our minds."

Stop with the "Yeah, Buts!"

Life is what we "perceive" it to be. Yet we will often hear "yeah, but" both from our inner voice and from others. Refuse to listen! If you look closely most of those "yeah, buts" come from critical and/or negative personalities; people who take comfort in seeing their limitations as "realism" and who look for validation in the actions of others.

Idealists, pessimists and realists all approach a challenge differently; the idealist's reality includes an answer, a way out, a way to overcome and achieve success, a new better reality. The idealist creates a new and better reality by trusting in the overall good and believing in the possibilities. Your own "yeah, but" is that mind of yours foolishly thinking it has to protect you from something that it does not understand; something that is perhaps outside your comfort zone.

Everyone has fears and doubts, even the most successful people. They just employ courage and take action anyway. You can, too! Lynn Pierce, founder of The Women's Business Empowerment Summit, taught in her book, *BREAKTHROUGH TO SUCCESS*, "Learn from your mistakes. It may not be the most fun way to learn, but truly successful people turn lemons into lemonade by finding the positive lesson in everything that happens." So, keep your recipe for lemonade handy and use it often. ☺

True Life Example: I published a trade magazine for interior designers and architects for five years. I was at a presentation, hoping to get a new advertiser. In becoming acquainted with a new company, I would inquire about their primary audience. This particular time their targeted market was the "general public," not interior designers and architects.

Now, I might have been able to convince the owner of the company I was speaking to that it would be good to broaden his market and include more advertising focus on interior designers. Instead, I replied, "You know, you're probably better off spending your money with XYZ magazine which effectively reaches the general public."

I ended up receiving a huge number of referrals from this prospect to people who did become advertisers. Why? He shared what I did, because it was unusual. I was trustworthy. Had I not had the courage to "lose" a client I would have lost many more! I had the courage to do the right thing.

Risk-Taking Can Be an Adventure

Now is a good time to reiterate Dr. Connell Cowan & Dr. Melvyn Kinder's powerful quote from their book, *WOMEN MEN LOVE WOMEN MEN LEAVE* , "Change can be frightening – it can also be an adventure – a growth-enhancing and empowering adventure – to experiment with new ways of being." I encourage you to have courage and experiment with new ways of being!

Do you have the courage to be your authentic, best and therefore happiest self? Do you feel you deserve to have what you really want in life? What stops you from achieving success and happiness?

How to Be Courageous

1. **Identify something that you want to do**, yet have not because you don't have the courage; something you have been meaning to do; something you have wanted to; yet were afraid to do.
2. **Eliminate confusion,** even if for just a little while. Find a quiet place, physically perhaps at first, but a place where after a few visits you can go in your mind even in the midst of confusion. It will be a safe haven, where with courage and wisdom you can listen to your intuition and discern a course of action.
3. **Ask yourself, why don't I do this thing?** Sometimes lack of courage shows up merely out of confusion and numbs our spirit leaving us in a false state of being a victim, a state that some try to justify as peaceful resignation.
4. **Ask yourself, what is the worst thing that might happen?** And, what's the worst thing about that? Realize that the lack of courage stems from fear and is something in your mind. Remember that FEAR stands for False Evidence Appearing Real. It is a belief you hold attached to an unsatisfactory outcome. Courage is the remedy for the many tricks our minds play on us.
5. **Ask yourself, what is the best thing that might happen? Start practicing accomplishing this in your mind**. It has been proven that when we practice in our mind we don't make mistakes. Envisioning and feeling a positive outcome or good result will always get us closer to success than envisioning failure.
6. **Finally, just do it!** There, you now have courage!

It takes courage to look at self-defeating habits. It takes courage to unpeel the layers hiding our core prosperity. It takes courage to decide we need to change, and it takes courage to stand by that decision. It takes courage to take the actions necessary to make necessary changes. Yet, as Maya Angelou told us, "Courage is the most important of all the virtues, because without courage you can't practice any other virtue consistently.

You can practice any virtue erratically, but nothing consistently without courage."

Please have the courage to use these Happiness Action Tools™ so you can live your happiest life. Trust me it is so worth it! I'm so glad I had the courage to change my life! For me it means no more hiding under the covers for days. Instead, I'm truly happy most of the time.

Jim Rohn told us, "Do battle with the enemy. Do battle with your fears. Build your courage to fight what is holding you back, what is keeping you from your goals and dreams. Be courageous in your life and in your pursuit of the things you want and the person you want to become."

How many successful moments in history happened because someone had the courage to take action? How many lives have seen saved because of courageous individuals?

Courage is paramount to our taking action and taking action is paramount to our achieving anything in life. Michael Ritter shared these inspiring words, **"Imagine what you could do if you weren't afraid to try."**

Vincent van Gogh expressed it in these words, "What would life be if we had not courage to attempt anything?" Have the courage to utilize the Happiness Action Tool™ of courage now to build your very happiest life so you get happy and stay happy.

Positive Expectation Statement™

For Happiness Action Tool™ #2
THE ENERGY OF COURAGE

"I am now actively courageous in life."

(7 words)

For free gifts to support you in being your happiest, visit your happiness community at TheHappinessCommunity.com.

CHAPTER FIVE

Find Your Touchstone

HAPPINESS ACTION TOOL™ #3

THE GIFT OF PURPOSE

"Keep away from people who try to belittle your ambitions.
Small people always do that,
but the really great make you feel that you, too can become great."
~ Mark Twain

"If we have our own 'why' of life, we can bear almost any 'how'."
~ Frederich Nietzsche

"Many persons have the wrong idea of what constitutes happiness.
It is not attained through self-gratification
but through fidelity to a worthy purpose."
~ Helen Keller

Have a purpose, or a reason, for living and you feel worthwhile and that your life matters. John Dewey said, "To find out what one is fitted to do, and to secure an opportunity to do it, is the key to happiness."

According to Napoleon Hill, "There is one quality that one must possess to win, and that is definiteness of purpose, the knowledge of what one wants, and a burning desire to possess it." Focusing on our own clear purpose builds a healthy sense of self-worth leading us to enhanced happiness. I believe we all have a gift to give to the world. We share that gift by first determining what it is and then by being true to ourselves in realizing our potential.

William Barclay put it like this, "There are two great days in a person's life – the day we are born and the day we discover why." Brian Tracy said, "Every single life only becomes great when the individual sets upon a goal or goals which they really believe in, which they can really commit themselves to, which they can put their whole heart and soul into."

There is a difference between purpose and function. Purpose is the why. Function is the what. Marie O'Conner told us, "It's not so much how busy you are, but why you are busy. The bee is praised; the mosquito is swatted." Purpose is **why** we do something. Function is **what** we do.

Once we know our purpose, we have a *reason* to pursue our goals: a *reason* to do what we need to. We naturally and easily express our true self. Knowing precisely what our purpose is, we are focused and, therefore, very persistent. We live our life with passion and enthusiasm. Even things not directly related to furthering our purpose have more meaning and are more pleasurable. We simply enjoy life more fully.

Katherine Hepburn said, "Life is to be lived. If you have to support yourself, you had bloody well better find some way that is going to be interesting."

Identify your purpose and see if the things you do fit into that basic purpose. Use it as a context and as a reference point to keep on target to building your best and happiest life.

Quentin Crisp had a humorous comment about this subject, "It's no good running a pig farm badly for thirty years while saying 'Really, I was meant to be a ballet dancer.' By that time, pigs are your style."

Purpose has been the subject of attention for ages. The theologians concerned themselves with what humanity's purpose was, hoping to give reason to life and to our individualization.

Margaret Young said, "Often people attempt to live their lives backwards: they try to have more things, or more money, in order to do more of what they want so they will be happier. The way it actually works is the reverse. You must first be who you really are, then do what you love to do, in order to have what you want."

"Having a purpose in your life is the most important element of becoming a fully functioning person," said Dr. Wayne Dyer. Having a purpose keeps us from being hopelessly scattered. Ralph Waldo Emerson expressed, "Where there is no vision, a people perish."

When you live your life on purpose, you love what you do. People resonate to that passion and commitment. They want to be with you, personally and in business. Ultimately, our purpose is to make our lives as happy as we possibly can. Michael Nolan expressed it well, "There are many things in life that will catch your eye, but only a few will touch your heart... pursue those."

Passion Fuels Purpose

Some people use the word passion to mean purpose. Yet, while they are important to each other, they are not the same. Passion fuels purpose.

Figuring out our unique gift(s) to the world holds the key to our purpose. **When we combine our gifts with passion, we effectively reflect our purpose**.

Knowing our purpose, we express our unique gifts which brings us happiness. Each of us has at least one unique gift to give life; a treasure to share that is all our own. These gifts come in many forms and expressed in many different ways. Once we identify what our special gifts are we will have a sense of purpose in our lives – a true feeling that our life is of value and has meaning.

Barbara Sher in her book, WISHCRAFT, described the difference having a purpose will make to our life. "If you are low on energy, if you need a lot of sleep and feel like you're always dragging yourself around at half throttle, it may not be because you need vitamins or have low blood sugar. It may be because you have not found your purpose in life. You will recognize your own path when you come upon it, because you will suddenly have all the energy and imagination you will ever need."

Ms. Sher went on to say, "This is part of the secret of all genuinely successful people: they have found their paths... but first you must liberate your own ingenuity and drive, and the only way to do that is to discover your own path; it is the only path that will ever truly absorb you. And the treasure at the end is success."

Jenny Craig shared, "You can't make serious money unless you love what you are doing! I've never met a successful person who hasn't been passionate about his work."

Concentrating on what's important builds healthy self-worth and self-esteem. The more we accomplish, the greater and stronger our sense of self-worth and corresponding happiness.

We All Have Gifts to Share

Looking at the gifts we have to share with life can assist in defining our life purpose. Although we may have many gifts to give life, usually one or two stand out and form the direction of our lives.

One of my gifts is my ability to assist people in understanding things. Another is my talent in being able to assist others in recognizing their specialness. Why look at that – I am truly utilizing two of my most significant gifts as I share this information with you.

True Life Example: The day I got in touch with my gift of being able to assist people in understanding things was very memorable. I was at a frustrating point in my life. I knew that I needed to direct my energies and feel more of a sense of accomplishment. I was just having trouble identifying how to go about that for myself.

I told my then husband how I envied his being so clear about his gift to life. Stan is an artist who expresses himself through the medium of photography. He has only doubted his purpose for rare fleeting moments. Even when he is frustrated, the idea of giving up photography truly does not enter his mind. He is one of the lucky people who have this clarity of their purpose in life.

Most of us aren't so clear about our own gifts and/or purpose. Sometimes someone else points it out to us. That's what happened to me. After my remark about envying his gift, Stan looked at me incredulously and said, "You mean you don't know what your gift to life is?" Sarcastically, I answered, "Now, if I knew what my gift was, would I be envying yours?" He laughed at me! He wasn't being cruel; it was clear to him. He explained to me "Your gift to life is your ability to help people understand things." I felt a sensation of my heart blossoming, and I knew he was right. And, here I am, writing this book sharing my gift and fulfilling my purpose.

You, too, can identify what your gift to life is. There are a number of ways to get in touch with this. It is important to know exactly what we want in life. How can we get something if we don't know what it is? So identifying our gift will help us set the course of our life!

The Touchstone of Our Dream

My friend, Patricia Clason, RCC, is Owner of Accountability Coaching Associates and Director for the Center for Creative Learning. Patricia is also a Professional Speaker, Author and Trainer in human resource development with over thirty years of experience. Patricia talks about the "touchstone" in our dreams.

She says that, **"the touchstone is the part of the dream that really motivates us."** It is what we identify with in the dream; it is *why* we want something. Patricia explains that within every dream there is something about it that is important, but it is not the career, the perfect house or the perfect outfit that is important.

The touchstone of our dream is about what happens when we have whatever it is or **how we feel when we have or are doing whatever it is**. What people seem to want is the object behind the object. We want the touchstone.

As we discussed, two of my touchstones are the sense of accomplishment and the sense of contribution. For me, expressing my gift to life by sharing through writing or speaking is a clear way for me to get both of those.

Barbara Sher also talks about dreams and touchstones in her book, *WISHCRAFT*. She says, "Your touchstone is the emotional core of your goal – what you want and need from it, what you love best about it. It's the sweet center of that goal for you."

She went on to say, "Creative fulfillment... fame... money... the chance to help people... closeness to nature... love – if you can put your touchstone into one or a few words, it will not only help you pick a target that's loaded with the kind of sweets that nourish you, it will also show you how to design the shortest, most direct and gratifying route to that goal, and it will get you to the essence of any goal that looks impossible."

As we discussed do be careful, however, not to mistake someone else's dream as your own. Once you are clear about your purpose; don't get distracted by other people's dreams or get caught up in their dreams or you may miss your own. Steve Jobs expressed it well, by saying **"We ought not to waste our lives by living someone else's.** We need all our energy for our own purpose and corresponding dreams."

We'll catch our own dreams by catching the wave of passion by being clear about our purpose. Let's take a minute here to look at the difference between dreams and purpose. Our dream may be our purpose, or it may only be a fleeting dream that we get caught up in. There is a difference. Pursue your purpose and your dreams will follow.

Chris Ensor stated, "Paint a portrait of life to be proud of, that could not be sold for all the money on earth. Hang that portrait in your mind and understand it's ever presence. Reflect on every brush stroke that makes all the mountains and valleys and rivers and skies the most beautiful in the land. Share your portrait with others but beware their brushes. Select only those whose brush will add to the beauty and structure of your masterpiece."

Ask yourself, "What would my life look like if I had all that I ever wanted?" Many clues will be in that picture.

Past Achievements Hold Clues

Our achievements hold good clues to our uniqueness and identifying our purpose. We have been demonstrating our strong qualities in what we have accomplished in our lives, which can assist us in identifying our touchstones.

Take credit for your accomplishments: no matter what they are. Each of us *is* accomplishing things in life, often, many more than we realize.

Some accomplishments are major. However, the many minor ones help us to achieve those larger ones. Recognize even these minor accomplishments for what they are: accomplishments. It doesn't matter what the level – it is still an accomplishment. Each one can motivate us to continue the journey of success.

You may insist that you have not achieved very much in life. You have. We have strong injunctions against taking credit for our actions, our strengths and our accomplishments.

It is uncomfortable for most of us to talk about our good qualities. Ask us to talk about our inadequacies and we can give you a list a mile long! Ask us to cite our attributes and we stammer incoherently. Not wanting to be considered vain, we downplay our strengths, even to ourselves.

Most of us believe modesty is a virtue; however, this twists the definition of modesty. The dictionary's definition of modesty is "having or showing a moderate estimation of one's own talents, abilities and value." The key word here is moderate. It doesn't say don't proudly estimate your own talents, abilities and value. It just says modesty is being "unpretentious," pretentious is "claiming or demanding a position of distinction or merit, especially when unjustified." The key word here is unjustified.

So, brag a little. Some people consider it negative to brag. Actually to brag is "to talk boastfully about oneself" and to boast is "to brag about one's own accomplishments, talents or possessions" and "to speak with pride." So, speak with pride about your talents, skills and accomplishments.

Here are some exercises you can use to identify your accomplishments and strengths so you can claim your personal "touchstones" and recognize your life purpose.

FIND YOUR TOUCHSTONE

Take it from me it really adds to your happiness in life if you are living on purpose! Wouldn't you like to get up every morning excited about how you are going to spend your day?

Getting to Know Me

Part I: Acknowledging Our Accomplishments

Here are a few guidelines: Don't attach judgments to perceived accomplishments. If you feel it is an accomplishment, it is. Every positive action we take is an accomplishment. However, for our purposes here we want to identify the ones that have significance for us. It is important to list things we feel are accomplishments; not necessarily, what the rest of the world would see as such. If an experience elicits approval from others yet doesn't mean anything to us, we aren't to include this in our list. We are looking for what motivates us, as well as what we are good at. To qualify as an achievement, it needs to be attached to a feeling you have of pride, joy or satisfaction.

1. **List at least 20 of your achievements**. Include your personal and family life, social and community activities, as well as your career. The list could consist of such things as passing your first test, getting your first job, losing weight, growing a vegetable garden, planning a special party, cooking a wonderful meal, earning a degree, running a marathon, or raising good children. We can each lay claim to accomplishments. Remember as far back as you can. There are no boundaries to this exercise. Many of our significant achievements were "firsts" for us. Remember, it's the feeling of accomplishment we are aiming at isolating here. Significant events often bring on this feeling. For instance, the feeling you had on your maiden solo bicycle voyage, when you answered a difficult question at school, your first athletic achievement.
2. **Narrow your list down to the top ten**. Start searching for clues.
3. **Look at why these are achievements for you.** What makes them important to you? How did you accomplish them? How did you feel? Can you identify the motivation or the outcome? In other words, did you feel a sense of love or sharing or a sense of contribution or a sense of accomplishment or a sense of power?
4. **Identify the common thread**. This will help you recognize your touchstones. How are they related? What threads can you identify? Are they mostly people-oriented, career-oriented, project-oriented or athletically oriented? What common feeling did they give you?

Part II: Recognizing Our Strengthens

Now we will look at recognizing our strengths, skills and aptitudes so we can meld those with our interests. The purpose of this is to identify our assets, our qualities, and our uniqueness. We are searching for our touchstones and our special gift(s) to life so we can live our life with the clarity of our purpose.

1. **List your skills**. What skills do you possess or have you learned? Can you type? Maybe you're good on the computer. Maybe you're good with power tools. Maybe you're skilled at repairing appliances, automobiles or machines. Maybe you design beautiful architecture or clothing. Or, maybe you're great at styling hair or caring for people's skin. Alternatively, maybe you know how to counsel others. Could be you're an expert at balancing accounts or budgeting. Perhaps you're excellent at public relations. Maybe you know how to handle a camera with ease. Everyone has skills. We just need to identify them. Just start listing them and watch the list grow.

2. **List your aptitudes**. What aptitudes or special talents do you have? Maybe you have a special talent for putting people at ease. Maybe you are good with numbers and figures. Maybe you are artistic. Maybe you have a special talent for organizing things or time or people. Maybe you are a take-charge person who can easily make decisions. Maybe you are good at doing things with your hands. Maybe you have the eye for detail work. On the other hand, maybe you have the patience to listen to others attentively. Maybe you love to write. Perhaps your talent is singing, dancing or performing. Could be that you have an investigative mind that helps to unravel mysteries, or maybe you have an analytical mind that allows you to solve problems. Again, it's just a process of identification.

Part III: Claiming Our Touchstones

1. **Recognize what you have identified as your touchstones** at this point and go with that. If this is not exactly right as you pursue this, your gifts and purpose will become clearer and clearer.
2. **Identify whether it is the thing itself or the lifestyle it will bring that you most want**. If it is just the lifestyle, strive to get that lifestyle doing what best fits with your touchstones.

My Life Purpose Statement

Use the following as a model and write out your purpose in life. Remember, this doesn't have to be written in stone; if you start following this avenue and it doesn't feel right, it is still valuable because it has led you toward what is right for you.

My gift to life and the world is:

My gift allows me to pursue my purpose in life of:

True Life Example: After I did this, I identified a couple of very apparent constants. As mentioned above, one was a sense of accomplishment and the other a sense of contribution. These threads tied all of my personal accomplishments together.

Here is my life purpose statement: "My purpose in life is to enhance people's self-esteem and happiness by utilizing my gift of assisting people to understand things and recognize their specialness." (And, that's just what's I'm doing! ☺)

Here is my writing partner (and friend) Linda Hancock Moore's life purpose statement: "My purpose in life is to live with passion, utilizing my gift of writing in projects of film or literature that heal with laughter, touch the heart, and lift the soul."

When we move toward our purpose fear falls away. Audre Lorde said it well, "When I dare to be powerful, to use my strength in the service of my vision, then it becomes less and less important whether I am afraid."

Nick Thornely put it this way, "Dreams are the most powerful motivators of all." John Wooden coached, "Do not let what you cannot do interfere with what you can do." Yet, as Dr. Denis Waitley said, "We've got to have a dream if we are going to make a dream come true."

Goals

Once we know our purpose, we can set goals to achieve our purpose. **Goals are the actions to take to manifest our purpose in life.** Goals are the plan to follow, direction to go, and roadmap to guide us. Goals are measurable, whereas purpose is ongoing.

Bob Proctor said, "Your purpose explains what you are doing with your life. Your vision explains how you are living your purpose. Your goals enable you to realize your vision."

Most people spend more time planning their vacations than planning the rest of their lives. You may have heard the expression, **"If you fail to plan, you're planning to fail**." Lee Iacocca said, "The discipline of writing something down is the first step toward making it happen." Harvey MacKay said, "A dream is just a dream. **A goal is a dream with a plan and a deadline**." *[Emphasis added.]*

Case Study: An interesting study of the 1953 Yale graduates validates the power of goal setting. Three percent (3%) of the students carried out comprehensive goal setting, 10% had modest and incomplete goal strategies, while 87% of the graduates had no goals at all.

Re-evaluating the study 20 years later showed that the three percent (3%) with comprehensive goals had accomplished more during that period than 97% of the other graduates *combined.* The income of the three percent (3%) group was 10 times more than that of the other 97%. Wow!

The secret to getting something is to see it in our mind's eye as complete and feeling you are doing or enjoying it. In other words, when we set a specific, measurable goal and **we believe we'll get it**, we will. You just need to be clear, specific and **expect** to get it.

There's real power in positive expectancy, remember? According to Benjamin Disraeli, "I have brought myself, by long meditation, to the conviction that a human being with a settled purpose must accomplish it, and that nothing can resist a will which will stake even existence upon its fulfillment."

True Life Example: Years ago, I had a car I really didn't like. I remember saying "That's okay; by the end of the year I will have $1000 to put down on a new sports car of my own." I really meant it. I certainly said it with a lot of conviction. I just knew it would happen. Well, guess what? On December 23rd of that year, I had $1000 for my new car.

Due to an unusual set of circumstances, although I did not have good credit, I found a banker who was willing to give me a loan. I thought I would have to get a "used car." However, remember I had said "new car." A conversation between the banker and the sales manager at the car dealership and I was approved for a loan for twice the original agreed upon amount – for a **new** sports car!

The reason this is so astounding is that I did nothing consciously to bring this about. I had forgotten about it. So, when it happened, just the way I said it would I analyzed why.

The most important reason was that I had believed it; I had expected it would happen! I had also been specific about what I would get, how much I would have to put down and when I would have it! We get what we want by asking specifically. So, ask big! Dr. Norman Vincent Peale said, "When you affirm big, believe big, and pray big, big things happen." Too bad, I didn't affirm bigger! ☺

True Life Example: Here's another amazing example. I wanted to go to Hawaii to visit my father and my 86-year-old grandmother who lived there. I set a 10-month goal. I knew I would go. I imagined myself boarding the plane, arriving and being greeted by my family.

I must confess that after setting this goal I again pretty much forgot about it. This time, however, I was not surprised when a month before my deadline I was given a ticket to Hawaii! Yes, I was **given** a free ticket. Again, I analyzed why I had achieved this goal. The components were the same as my other "miracle." I had set a goal that was clear, specific with a deadline. I had believed and expected it would happen.

Goal Setting is Vital to Success

Goal setting is vital to success. I have been studying the actions of successful people for many years and one thing they have in common it is a belief in goal setting. Setting guidelines for yourself assists you in attaining your aims, knowing where you are headed, and how you plan to get there and when you plan to arrive. James Allen said, "You will become as great as your dominant aspiration... if you cherish a vision in your heart, you will realize it."

Here are a few more motivating quotes about pursuing your purpose in life. Barry Munre said, "You are only as strong as your purpose, therefore let us choose reasons to act that are big, bold, righteous and eternal."

Samuel Goldwyn said, "No person who is enthusiastic about his work has anything to fear from life. All the opportunities in the world are waiting to be grasped by people who are in love with what they are doing."

Here are a few more motivating quotes about pursuing your purpose in life. Barry Munre said, "You are only as strong as your purpose, therefore let us choose reasons to act that are big, bold, righteous and eternal."

Samuel Goldwyn said, "No person who is enthusiastic about his work has anything to fear from life. All the opportunities in the world are waiting to be grasped by people who are in love with what they are doing."

Again, I share a quote from Dale Carnegie, "Are you bored with life? Then throw yourself into some work you believe in with all your heart, live for it, die for it, and you will find happiness that you thought could never be yours."

Keep your dream in **ONE CUP** only – not two. Don't have an everyday cup and a dream cup that you keep on the shelf that you only bring down on occasion to share with a guest. Put something in your one cup, no matter how big or how small, every single day and you will become the cup that "runneth over" with an abundant life full of continued possibilities, well-being and happiness.

Here's a lighter quote from an unknown writer, "To love what you do and feel that it matters – how could anything be more fun?" Lovely actress and savvy minded, Susan Sarandon, who's still radiant and going strong, said upon turning 40, "I've redefined success for myself to mean being happy when doing exactly what I do."

George Bernard Shaw expressed, "**This is the true joy in life, the being used for a purpose recognized by yourself as a mighty one**; the being thoroughly worn out before you are thrown on the scrap heap; the being a force of nature instead of a feverish selfish little clod of ailments and grievances complaining that the world will not devote itself to making you happy." *[Emphasis added.]*

Goal Setting

1. **Set the goal** – one that is ambitious and yet attainable.
2. **Make sure it is specific, measurable, and believable.** Be sure to have a date of completion.
3. **Make a list of the benefits** for achieving your goal.
4. **Imagine and feel the goal as if you have attained it.** Read the chapter on visualization for help with this one.
5. **Remind yourself regularly of the benefits** you will get by accomplishing your goal.

With your touchstone, you have a reason to live. Goal setting gives you the roadmap to follow. so go and be all God intended you to be! What is your big picture for life? A clear and challenging vision will always draw you upwards. Besides, you don't want to be like Jane Wagner and end up saying, "All my life I wanted to be somebody. But I see now I should have been more specific." Go live your purposeful happiest life!

Positive Expectation Statement™

For Happiness Action Tool™ #3
THE GIFT OF PURPOSE

"I live my life on purpose."

(6 words)

CHAPTER SIX

Whisper Sweet Somethings...

HAPPINESS ACTION TOOL™ #4

THE IMPACT OF SELF-TALK

"The more man meditates upon good thoughts,
the better will be his world and the world at large."
~ Confucius

"He who would be useful, strong, and happy
must cease to be a passive receptacle
for the negative, beggarly, and impure streams of thought;
and as a wise householder commands his servants
and invites his guests,
so must he learn to command his desires and to say,
with authority, what thoughts he shall admit
into the mansion of his soul."
~ James Allen

"If you hear a voice within you say 'you cannot paint,'
then by all means paint, and that voice will be silenced."
~ Vincent van Gogh

Listen carefully to what you say to yourself because what you say to yourself is very, very important. For instance, when I say, "What do I know?" I now answer myself with "Plenty!"

What we allow ourselves to hear in our mind molds our life. You heard that right, I said, "allow." What we say to ourselves becomes our destiny, determining what happens in our life.

Frank Outlaw said it so well, "Watch your thoughts, they become words. Watch your words, they become actions. Watch your actions, they become habits. Watch your habits they become character. Watch your character, it becomes your destiny."

Self-talk is the conversation we have with ourselves. It is our inner dialogue. As we go about our day, we make comments to ourselves about almost everything. Whether we are aware of it or not we talk to ourselves almost constantly.

Many of us have adopted negative attitudes we hold onto and perpetuate instead of adopting attitudes that are more positive. While that's the bad news, the good news is that **we can change our mind**. We can take control and decide what we think and what we tell ourselves. Dr. Denis Waitley said, "Relentless, repetitive self talk is what changes our self-image."

Grace Jasmine revealed, "You can alter the state of your mind, or attitude, as simply as you alter your body. Just as a daily plan of exercise and nutrition will keep your body healthy, a daily plan of positive affirmation and visualization will keep your mind, and your attitude healthy."

She went on to say, "The concepts of affirmation and visualization are simple ones, and although the theory is quite easy to master, it is the consistent application that will enable you to truly change your attitude."

The person that we talk to the most every day is our self. **The most important things that are said "to" us are said "by" us.** Do you nurture and encourage yourself, or most often put yourself down and say negative, critical things?

What you say to yourself can be the difference between your success and failure. You can be either your own worst critic or your own best cheerleader.

Catherine Ponder in *THE DYNAMIC LAWS OF PROSPERITY* expressed, **"Never underestimate the power of words. You make your world with your words."**

Ms. Ponder further added, "From counseling hundreds of people with financial problems, I have found that 99 times out of 100 they do not solve their problems until they not only know, but fully use the law of command. **When they begin daily, consciously, and deliberately to assert the good they want, their commands seem to call it forth."**

WHISPER SWEET SOMETHINGS...

Learn to listen to your higher consciousness, not to the negative "mind chatter" that goes on and on from our negative programming. The good things we learned as a child, as well as the negative things, are like tapes that play again, and again, in our head. They will continue to play repeatedly until we have the courage to stop them by replacing them with more constructive, helpful, loving and supportive thoughts.

Unfortunately, most of us need a life changing experience to get our attention long enough to decide we need to change. Don't ignore the signs in your life that signal you to consider change by taking responsibility to "re-think" your thinking.

Joe Robson shared with us, "Our first attempts to speak were unintelligible to others, but we weren't born with a negative inner voice telling us we'd never communicate like adults. So why do we worry so much about our occasional adult failures? I believe that if we hadn't cultivated that negative inner voice, human kind would now be populating those far off stars we now dream of reaching."

T. Harv Eker in his book *SECRETS OF THE MILLIONAIRE MIND* wrote, "In our courses we teach that 'no thought lives in your head rent-free.' Each thought you have will be either an investment, or a cost. It will either move you toward happiness and success or away from it. It will either empower you or disempower you. That's why it is imperative you choose your thoughts and beliefs wisely."

To get complimentary tickets to Harv Eker's three-day Millionaire Mind Seminar, the one that positively changed my life visit http://www.peakambassador.com/cmd.php?af=mmi21066&p=1 or you can call 888.868.8883 and use my reference ID#mmi21066. It's truly a fabulous seminar.

90,000 Thoughts a Day

We have as many as 90,000 thoughts and receive about 600,000 bits of information in a day! Many of these are the same ones repeated; however, that is still a lot of thoughts. If most of those thoughts are negative, how dangerous is that?

WHISPER SWEET SOMETHINGS...

One of my favorite books is by James A. Takacs called *YOUR MIND CAN DRIVE YOU CRAZY (ONLY IF YOU LET IT)*. Mr. Takacs said, "The human mind is the most complicated, sophisticated, versatile and powerful data bank in existence. Feeding this tremendous vault of information are various senses, i.e., touch, smell, auditory, visual and memories of past sensations, which involve all of these. Every day we process those 600,000 bits of such information usually in the form of words since this is our form of communication."

He went on to say, "During a normal day we utilize approximately 24,000 words to communicate our thoughts, which is only a small fraction of our thoughts; only a small fraction of our daily input. You see, you are communicating ideas for both good and bad, and the words you use have a very definite effect upon your life."

Talk is verbalized thinking and those 90,000 thoughts that we have everyday can help us to gauge our attitude. We can then change our life by changing our words. It truly is that simple: different input, different output. Pay attention to that constant chatter in your head – it can be either your best friend or your worst enemy!

Dr. Robert Anthony expressed it well, "The way you talk to yourself has a profound effect upon your feelings, actions and accomplishments. What you say determines practically everything you do. For instance, **words can even change blood pressure, heartbeat and breathing**." *[Emphasis added.]*

He further said, "The **subconscious mind accepts without question the words we use to program it**, whether they are positive or negative. Positive statements or affirmations build your life while negative statements or affirmations destroy. Take a moment right now to think about this." *[Emphasis added.]*

He added, "What you must do is police your speech and turn such self-defeating statements around. The way to program your mind is to use positive affirmations and repeat them repeatedly until your subconscious accepts them as reality. In psychology, this is the Law of Predominate Mental Impression.

When you keep saying that you are sick, your subconscious is required to make you sick; if you affirm health, it is required to make you healthy."

He went on to say, "Be careful not to create a contrary situation by saying to yourself that you feel great, then, the next minute when someone asks how you are, telling them you feel terrible just to get their sympathy. Switching back and forth only confuses the subconscious, and this will have repercussions in your life."

Our subconscious mind does not know the difference between fact and fiction. It is as if our brain is a computer. (We talked about this in the introduction, too – this is just important information.) It only knows what we tell it. So, monitor the input; feed it positive data to get positive output.

Mr. Takacs added, "Remember your subconscious is your obedient, 'Yes Boss' servant. When you say, 'I have this drinking problem' or 'I have a terrible cold' your mind simply agrees with you. Don't feed your mind negative garbage! Feed it positive thought!"

He encouraged us, "Before you set about to dismantle your own conning tower, to remove the source of negativity, let me give you a better idea. All you need do is alter how you use it. Use it to 'con' yourself in a positive direction."

Should is a Useless Word

Please, do not take an action because you think you "**should**." **Should** is a useless word. I would like to see it eliminated from the English language. Think about it. Who says you **should** and why **should** you? Okay, you say, "I **should** eat healthier." Who says so, and why?

It would be more appropriate to say, "I would feel better if I ate healthier." Can you feel the difference in the strength of that statement, and therefore its effectiveness? The attached benefit gives the statement power. "

"Should statements" are parental and outside of us – we are not in power. If anything, when we hear the word **should**, it is our tendency to rebel. Start noticing how often you **should** yourself. Instead, **give yourself benefit statements that will motivate you to accomplish what you are aiming for**.

Benefit statements, on the other hand, are positive and motivate us because we can see and/or feel the good that will come from them. Change the word **should** to **want**. If you hear yourself saying, "I **should** clean my room." Change that to, "I **want** to clean my room." Can you feel the difference?

Be Careful, Be Very Careful

What most people call "affirmations" I refer to as a "Positive Expectation Statement™." Remember, we get what we expect in life. What we say creates a positive or a negative expectation.

True Life Example: I used to think it was clever to tell people, "I don't plan to have children until I can afford a nanny so they will only see Mommy when she is in a good mood." Now, that might be a clever expression, but remember our subconscious does not know the difference between fact and fiction.

Guess who couldn't afford a nanny until it was too late? This was anything but how I really felt. I adore children and I would have been a wonderful mother. Did I really care about my children only seeing me in a good mood? No! However, my subconscious believed what I told it; what it heard repeatedly.

True Life Example: Here is another even more startling example. An expression I began using as a teen that I also thought was cute was, "Since the first half of my life was so lousy the second half is going to be great!" Well, the lousiness continued for many more years so I've added, "I just didn't know that I was going to grow to be so old!"

The reality is that my subconscious held me back from experiencing true happiness for many years because of those words I used. The good news is that I know I get to live to a very ripe old age – because, as you now understand, I have convinced my subconscious I will. ☺

WHISPER SWEET SOMETHINGS...

Jim Rohn shared that, "If you spend five minutes complaining, you have just wasted five minutes. If you continue complaining, it won't be long before they haul you out to a financial desert and there let you choke on the dust of your own regret."

How You See Yourself

True Life Example: I used to use the words "fighter" and "survivor" often to describe myself. One would think these are positive words. Well, I realized that fighters "fight battles" and survivors "just get by." Wow! I looked at my life – and guess what? I was always fighting a battle and just getting by.

I decided to change those two words and came up with one word to replace both. From then on when I heard myself saying, I am a fighter or a survivor I would say, "THAT MAY HAVE BEEN TRUE IN THE PAST, however **I am now a happy THRIVER**." For me, that word is very positive – it brings up pictures of green, lush, growing living plants.

Take the action of following the instructions in *HOW YOU SEE YOURSELF* to find what words you use that let you know how you see yourself. Be aware that your interpretation of these, or any, words is your own. We all see the world through our own perspective. A word that might be okay for you may not be effective for someone else.

Following the instructions in *HOW YOU SEE YOURSELF* will help you identify the words you use to describe yourself; words your mind hears repeatedly. It will be more effective if you use words that will impact *your* life positively.

You can choose to change the words you now use to words you resonate with that make you feel good. I suggest you then create Positive Expectation Statements™ using your power words to assist you in building your happiest life.

Here's a challenge for you. For at least the next 24 hours, carefully listen to yourself and replace your limiting statements with your new Positive Expectation Statements™.

How You See Yourself

This is effective in helping to recognize how we see ourselves and how that relates to how we function in the world. This can be life changing!

1. **Divide a piece of paper into 3 vertical columns**.
2. **List 10 words** down the center that you use to describe yourself. Don't think about the words – just write them quickly as them come to you. **Don't judge the words** (you'll understand why in a few minutes). Leave a couple of spaces between each word.
3. **Write down what's "not good" about your word in the left column** about the attribute that's in the center column. What is **your** definition of this word from a (your) negative perspective?
4. **Write down what "is good" about your word in the right column** about the attribute that's in the center column. What is **your** definition of this word from a (your) positive perspective?
5. **Repeat 3 & 4** for each of your words in the center column.
6. **Rewrite your list of words** – to words that you would like to have as attributes of yourself. Would replacing a word better fit how **you** would like to see you and how you relate to **your** world?
7. **Create a Positive Expectation Statement**™ utilizing the tool, The Power of Six, to replace the limiting word(s) you have identified and then use this every time you hear yourself using your "soon-to-be-old" limiting and prohibitive self-talk.
8. **Accept this as the truth** for yourself by posting the new list where you can view it often.

Don't Argue with Yourself

Oh, and please don't argue with yourself. It is important not to input negativity. I must emphasize how important this is. Remember our brains are like computers.

Computers don't understand an argument – they do, however, understand replacing one file with another. The computer simply overrides the one with the other. So in replacing our negative sentence with a positive one "our computer" will accept the corrected sentence as the new fact.

Positive Expectation Statements™

I coined the term Positive Expectation Statements™ for what others may call affirmations because I feel this is a more powerful description. I have created a tool that utilizes these statements in a very effective manner.

It's best to create your Positive Expectation Statement™ utilizing at least six and no more than eight words. There is a reason for the number of words. I heard it takes six positives to negate one negative. In other words for each negative statement we need to replace it six times. Seems that six is some kind of magic number for that computer we call our brain.

How to Implement The Power of Six explains how to create and use your own Positive Expectation Statements™. Allowing up to eight words allows for flexibility and yet keeps the statement short enough for you to remember easily, and therefore encourages its repetition.

How to Implement The Power of Six Tool

The idea is to create a positive statement to replace any negative statement. We want to create a Positive Expectation Statement™ utilizing six to eight words to make this easy to implement.

It might be easy to start with the basic Positive Expectation Statement™: "I am now experiencing perfect __________." (You add whatever word you want to replace the negative thought.) For instance, if you hear yourself saying, "I think I'm getting a cold," you would say, "I am now experiencing perfect health" at least six times.

Here's what makes this simple. The above statement is six words. If you emphasize each word in order, you can easily repeat your Positive Expectation Statement™ six times. Here's an example:

1. **I** am now experiencing perfect health.
2. I **AM** now experiencing perfect health.
3. I am **NOW** experiencing perfect health.
4. I am now **EXPERIENCING** perfect health.
5. I am now experiencing **PERFECT** health.
6. I am now experiencing perfect **HEALTH**.

The statement could be about wealth, happiness, intelligence, or any positive word(s). Replace the word "perfect" with another positive word if you like. Just have it be at least six words. You can use any six words that work for you. However sticking to a basic script will help you do it spontaneously, quickly and easily.

In the Now

It is important to phrase our Positive Expectation Statements™ **as if they are happening now**. The computer that is your brain will more readily accept your statement as fact. It will accept it as if it is already a reality now and your output will reflect this.

Be very careful of what words you are using in your life. Decide to use Positive Expectation Statements™ to create a new reality for your life and then act on that decision. Carefully choose the words to use in manifesting a new destiny for yourself.

Speaking of choosing your words carefully I encourage you to create Positive Expectation Statements™ that you resonate with. Create them so they emotionally charge you!

My Favorite Positive Expectation Statements™

I have a few favorite Positive Expectation Statements™ I repeat every day upon awakening and every night before sleeping. I memorized them before I created the POWER OF SIX.

The first is the Serenity Prayer, which I have revised slightly by adding a couple words that I think gives it even more power:

> "God grant me the serenity to accept the things I cannot change, the courage [and resources] to change the things I can, and the wisdom to know the difference to know the difference."

The other is from a very old UNIT DAILY WORD. I'm sure it's not exactly the same now as I'm sure I've customized it over the years. The words surrounded by brackets [ ] are words I have I know I've added for greater power. Here it is:

> "I am thankful that nothing can stand in the way of the good that God has for me [not even me]. Nothing can stand in the way or prevent the free flow of that which is my divine birthright. I am kept calm and serene by my faith in the power of God to adjust all circumstances and to bring about that which is for the highest good of all concerned. The people I need to meet and know and who need to meet and know me are right now are on their way. We are divinely drawn to one another. God wills only good for me. I affirm the good that seeks recognition expression in my life. I affirm the good. I look for only good and happy outcomes

> in all things and I give thanks that nothing can stand in the way of that good! [Not even me!]"

This one is from the book THE DYNAMIC LAWS OF PROSPERITY by Catherine Ponder. My mother greatly admired Catherine Ponder and she often read to us from THE DYNAMIC LAWS OF PROSPERITY so we used to call it "Our 2nd Bible." I sincerely wish I could meet her to tell her how much she influenced our family. Here are her words:

> "I am now experiencing perfect health, abundant prosperity and complete and utter happiness. This is true because the world is full of charming people who lovingly help me in every way. I am now come into an innumerable company of angels. I am now living a delightful interesting and satisfying life of the most widely useful kind. Because of my own increased health, wealth and happiness, I am now able to help others live a delightful, interesting and satisfying life of the most widely useful kind. My good – our good – is universal."

There Are No Problems

True Life Example: Here are a few words to consider replacing. Instead of the word "problem," Try "creative challenge" because all problems have solutions for resolving them. Thus, it is not a "problem;" it is a challenge that with a corresponding solution. Some people also refer to a "pending solution."

My friend, Tod Spence, said an ex-boss taught him to use the word "opportunity" instead of problem. Because he had to practice this on the job, it became something that changed his entire life. He says it was the best gift he ever received.

You may say this is just semantics. However, our brain responds better to positive input. No meaningful goal is without obstacles. View these "obstacles" as "challenges" or "opportunities" that are part of the journey to success and see them favorably.

Compliment Yourself Often and Profusely

Indulge in positive self-talk often. Tell yourself often how worthy you are, how very special you are and how much you would be missed. In other words, compliment yourself often and profusely. Say "Good-Bye" and "Good Riddance" to your internal critic. You will learn to think a new language, not just speak it.

Ah, the impact of positive self-talk! Be our own best cheerleader. Whisper sweet somethings in your ear and feel the impact of self-talk in living your happiest life.

Positive Expectation Statement™

For Happiness Action Tool™ #4
THE IMPACT OF SELF-TALK

"I fill my head with positive thoughts."

(7 words)

For a **free** comprehensive list of Positive Expectation Statements™ and other gifts to support you in being your happiest, visit TheHappinessCommunity.com.

CHAPTER SEVEN

Ignore Peripheral Distractions

HAPPINESS ACTION TOOL™ #5
THE CLARITY OF FOCUS

"Where you are headed is more important than how fast you are going. Rather than always focusing on what's urgent, learn to focus on what is really important."
~ Unknown Author

"Concentration is the secret of strength."
~ Ralph Waldo Emerson

"Focus is everything. If only we had a way to teach it, that would be an education extraordinaire!"
~ William James

Focus backed by intent is like magic. Abraham Hicks said, "Genius is nothing more than focus on a thing." Intent is a mysterious magnetic force behind the unseen workings of universal law. It is our intent that sets our lives in motion determining what kind of life we live.

When we focus, we unleash the impact of that intent. What we focus on manifests and creates our happiness, or when negatively applied, our unhappiness.

An unknown author said, "Success is never an accident. It's the result of passion, sincere intention, effort and action."

What are you focusing on? Where are you directing your energy? What is your intent? Are your intentions the highest kind – or are they selfishly focused on material gain?

Reverend Neil Colton said, "Don't focus on the negative things in life, when there are options. Negative energy breeds negative energy. Positive energy breeds positive energy." As Reverend Colton pointed out, we have options; we can choose what we focus on.

However, before we decide what we will focus on, we must determine our intent. We can be part of creating a better world, or we can just concentrate on our own selfish desires, with little or no heed to how it affects the world. As Reverend Colton shared, we attract back the same energy we send out, whether it be positive or negative energy.

Having an intention to make lots of money may result in your making lots of money however, that does not guarantee you happiness. Having an intention to live your life to the fullest, in peace and joy, will make you rich internally, which affects everything else you endeavor to do, including financial success.

Everything is Energy

Understand that everything is made of energy, which means our intentions are energy. **Energy is always in motion sending a ripple effect that sets into motion a chain of events that affects the entire universe. Our thoughts, both conscious and unconscious, direct energy; we are the driving force. Therefore, we create our experiences and our lives.**

We discuss the theory that our inner world creates our outer world many times. **We can choose to become conscious creators by focusing our thoughts and intentions.** This is the essence of what the book *THE SECRET* teaches.

Loretta Staples shared, "If you are clear about what you want, the world responds with clarity." Lack of focus is one of the most significant reasons people do not get what they want in life.

No matter what you want, focusing will help you achieve it. When you are focused you don't let anything or anyone get in your way. You have a strong will. You are resolved to accomplish your desire; you are determined. You have more control over your life. Nido Quebin said, "Nothing can add more power to your life than concentrating all your energies on a limited set of targets."

IGNORE PHERIPERAL DISTRACTIONS

Fear interrupts focus and clouds the issue. Life really is too short not to be awake and aware. James Allen told us, "The more tranquil a man becomes, the greater is his success, his influence, his power for good. Calmness of mind is one of the beautiful jewels of wisdom." Brian Tracy proclaimed, **"The key to success is to focus our conscious mind on things we desire not things we fear."**

We all know people with big visions and dreams that never seem to come to fruition because of lack of focus. Marsha Sinetar expressed, "Life's strict rule is this: You get more of what you focus on. Ignoring this, we abandon our healthiest, concentrative energies and court emotional upheaval."

Norman Vincent Peale revealed, "When every physical and mental resource is focused, one's power to solve a problem multiplies tremendously." An unknown author shared, "The successful man is the average man, focused."

T. Harv Eker, in *SECRETS OF THE MILLIONAIRE MIND*, expressed, "It's simple. Your field of focus determines what you find in life. Focus on opportunities and that is what you find. Focus on obstacles and that is what you find."

He further clarified, "I'm not saying you don't take care of problems. Of course, handle problems as they arise, in the present. Just keep your eye on your goal. Keep moving toward your target. Put your time and energy into creating what you want."

He added, "When obstacles arise, handle them, and then quickly refocus on your vision. You do not make your life about solving problems. You do not spend all your time fighting fires. Those who do, move backward! You spend your time and energy in thought and deed, moving steadily forward, toward your goal."

Enthusiastically Concentrate Your Energies

Daniel Meacham gave this wise advice, "Concentrate all your energies on the task or situation at hand. You have at your disposal the two most marvelously devised and efficient machines ever created; the human body and the human mind. When used correctly, they can work wonders. They can move mountains. **You** can move mountains."

He further expressed, "Like a sprinter surging toward the finish line, focus every particle of yourself on your objective. Don't look back; surge ahead!" An unknown author expressed, "Live life with a fire that is never extinguished."

What we are talking about here is, of course, **passion, which coupled with clear and sincere intent, is very powerful**. Direct all of your energy in one direction. It is the highest form of paying attention and being present. Focusing is powerful. It allows us to accomplish more in less time. We magnify the results by focusing, by being specific. The more specific and clear our intent the more powerful and the quicker it will manifest.

Focus creates the most satisfying outcome in the shortest amount of time. "What I focus on in life is what I get. And if I concentrate on how bad I am or how wrong I am or how inadequate I am, if I concentrate on what I can't do and how there's not enough time to do it, isn't that what I get every time? And when I think about how powerful I am, and when I think about what I have left to contribute, and when I think about the difference I can make on this planet, then that's what I get. You see, I recognize that's not what happens to you; it's what you do about it," shared W. Mitchell.

There is no definitiveness on how or when our desired intent will manifest. Our personal beliefs and doubts, fears and blocks – or lack thereof – determines the speed of outcome. Focusing on your intent with clarity *will* produce the desired result.

Goethe expressed, "Until one is committed, there is hesitancy, the chance to draw back, always ineffectiveness. Concerning all acts of initiative there is one elementary truth, the ignorance of which kills countless ideas and splendid plans: that the moment one definitely commits oneself then Providence moves too. All sorts of things occur to help one that would otherwise never have occurred. A whole stream of events issues from the decision, raising in one's favor all manner of incidents and meetings and material assistance which no person would have believed would have come their way." (Isn't Goethe wonderful?)

Have you noticed that when inspired you feel focused? It is as if a great spirit outside of you gives you a sense of purpose or a calling. When you are inspired, it is easy to stay focused. Just remember to check your focus from time to time. Is this in line with your intent?

True Life Example: An aspiring actor was asked if her dream was about the acting itself or the lifestyle that is associated with being an actor. She explained that it wasn't until years later that she understood the full impact of that question. She explained it came back to her while watching Whoopi Goldberg in an interview on *INSIDE ACTORS STUDIO* with James Lipton.

One of the students in the audience said she had heard Ms. Goldberg say that anyone who sincerely wanted to be a successful actor could become one. The student wanted to know if she meant what she had said, or was she just saying it out of encouragement. Whoopi replied that she had been sincere. However, she went on to explain that one would be better not confusing becoming a dedicated actor with becoming a "celebrity." It is our intention that sets the course, and focus and discipline bring our intent into being.

Focus on Happiness Today

Awareness and focus are two closely related words. **Focus is being able to do something without distraction**. Awareness means we pay attention. The dictionary definition is "having knowledge or cognizance." For the purpose of this book I think of "awareness" as the critical condition for "focus," because of its' ability to put us "fully in the present moment," to truly **BE HERE NOW.**

True Life Example: A friend commented that I have a great ability to be "present." What he meant was that I really live in the moment. No matter what outside pressures may affect my life I am able to focus on the "present" and "be here now."

I have not always been able to do that. I am human and occasionally have a bad hour; however that is usually all I allow myself anymore. I no longer suffer through entire days of hiding under the covers because I was focusing on my unknown future and creating fear.

Being able to focus on the present was a great aspiration for me. Having a friend recognize that I had accomplished this and tell me I had achieved this great goal was a significant moment in my life.

In the movie, *FIELD OF DREAMS*, there is a line about how we often miss the most significant moments of our lives while they are happening. Most of us spend so much time looking backward or forward we miss today. We either are busy regretting the past or caught up in looking ahead to the better life that awaits us. Let's keep making that effort to find happiness in the present.

James Dillet Freeman in *UNITY MAGAZINE* wrote, "We should keep in mind that it is now and only now that we are alive, and if longing for the past or hoping for the future dominates too much of our thinking, we may find that neither past nor future has much pleasure in it, for it is only as we live richly now that we build a life of joyous memories and prepare for future growth and unfoldment."

He further said, "Today contains the substance of the past and the essence of the future; it is only out of todays and in terms of todays that yesterdays and tomorrows find reality. The new year will be full of old joys and new thrills as we live each day as joyfully and thrillingly as we are able, whatever circumstances today may happen to contain."

We want to be happy every day, not just when we "arrive." As Greg Anderson said, "Focus on the journey, not the destination."

Happiness can be found as much in doing an activity as finishing it. We can enjoy the clarity of focus by concentrating on the one most important thing at any given time.

As Linda Hancock Moore shared, "Multi-tasking may be a talent, but being able to focus rules!"

IGNORE PHERIPERAL DISTRACTIONS

Shiny Object Syndrome

While multi-tasking can be helpful sometimes, chasing multiple shiny objects or running from one shiny object to another is not helpful. In fact, it's a way to literally drive yourself crazy. At the very least, shiny object syndrome will leave us with many unfinished projects, lost income and maximum frustration. Pick one lovely shiny object you can feel passionate about and focus on that one, and only that one, insuring you give it all you can!

How to Focus

1. **Clear away all distractions,** physically and mentally. Sometimes it's difficult to eliminate the distractions, so you have to do it mentally by tuning out the noise around you.
2. **Be clear about the task.** Envision and feel the result. Break it into manageable steps and start with one at a time.
3. **Stay in the present.** Stay focused on each step until you reach your goal. Do not let your peripheral vision startle or distract you.

Life doesn't just happen to us. It's about the choices we make along the way. **We create and magnify what we focus on**. This happens every day, all day.

I'd again like to quote Goethe, "The moment one definitely commits oneself then Providence moves too. All sorts of things occur to help one that would otherwise never have occurred." I encourage you to definitely commit to focusing on living your happiest life.

Positive Expectation Statement™

For Happiness Action Tool™ #5
THE CLARITY OF FOCUS

"I consciously focus on being happy."

(6 words)

For gifts to support you in being your happiest, visit your happiness community at TheHappinessCommunity.com.

CHAPTER EIGHT

No Fairy Godmother Required

HAPPINESS ACTION TOOL™ #6

THE POWER OF PERSPECTIVE

"The greatest discovery of my generation is that human beings, by changing the inner attitudes of their minds, can change the outer aspects of their lives."
~ William James

"Each experience through which we pass operates ultimately for our good... This is a correct attitude to adopt... and we must be able to see it in that light."
~ Orison Swett Marden

"There are two ways to live your life ... One is as though nothing is a miracle, The other is as though everything is a miracle."
~ Albert Einstein

Think yourself happy! Yes, you can think yourself happy. Happiness is an attitude. "We either make ourselves miserable, or happy and strong. The amount of work is the same," shared Francesca Reigler.

Perspective determines our beliefs; and our beliefs, in turn, determine our attitude. One definition of attitude is "a feeling or emotion toward a fact or state of being."

Therefore, our thought determines our feeling and, our feeling determines our actions. Perspective is vital to our happiness as it determines our beliefs and our attitude.

Attitude is More Important Than Facts

Virginia Satir shared, "**Life is not the way it's supposed to be. It is the way it is. The way you cope with it is what makes the difference.**" She noted, "I think if I have one message, one thing before I die that most of the world would know, it would be that **the event does not determine how to respond to the event.** That is a purely personal matter. The way in which we respond will direct and influence the event more than the event itself." *[Emphasis added.]*

We may not be responsible for the action; however, we are responsible for our reaction. It is not whether good things or bad things happen to us. It is how we interpret what happens. We are in charge of our reaction and our attitude. It's all in our perspective. Whether we see things negatively or positively we experience corresponding negative or positive outcomes. Lee Piper said, "The mind cannot be trusted. **We can think ourselves into anything**." *[Emphasis added.]*

Earl Nightingale proclaimed, "A great attitude does much more than turn on the lights in our worlds; it seems to magically connect us to all sorts of serendipitous opportunities that were somehow absent before the change." I found this quote on ivillage.com, "Think happiness happens by luck or chance? Not so! **The truth is that you can cultivate a happy and positive outlook on life – no fairy godmother required**." *[Emphasis added.]*

True Life Example: On special occasions, my mother would have us gather several hours before dinner. She, of course, just wanted to have us with her longer, however everyone got quite hungry and, therefore, irritable. We would all sit down to eat and everyone would be grouchy and complaining. I would always get an upset stomach and be unable to finish my dinner.

Realizing the dynamics of this, I chose to change my perspective, which in turn changed the perspective and the behavior of my brothers. Here's what happened. One evening we sat down to dinner and the bickering began. I calmly ate my food. I deliberately looked up, made eye contact with each of my three brothers at the table, and said, "Wow! This food is so delicious. The rest of you could choose to enjoy it, too." And, I went back to enjoying my dinner. An unusual silence came over the room and everyone else began eating, too! I later explained to my mother what had occurred. She began to prepare snacks for us to enjoy, which helped control the irritableness from our low blood sugars. I chose to stop being part of the chaos. What do you want to change?

There are a number of maxims about perspective. "Two men looked through prison bars; one saw mud, the other saw stars," says an old English rhyme. I have also heard that, "Happiness isn't having what we want; it's wanting what we have."

The wonderful Helen Keller, with all of her physical challenges, proved that we can rise above and that happiness is attainable. She said, "When one door of happiness closes, another opens; but often we look so long at the closed door that we don't see the one that has been opened for us."

Attitude is more important than facts. It is more important than our past, how much money we have, how much education we have, and even more important than circumstances. It is more important than what other people think, say, or do. It is more important than how beautiful or handsome we are and more important than our talents or skills. **Our attitude determines almost everything, and is one of the biggest factors in our determining our happiness.**

It's Just Spaghetti

True Life Example: Here's a fun story about how our attitude determines our reaction. Cindy Stanphill worked at an Italian restaurant. One evening they were short staffed and things were hectic so the staff was getting uptight. Suddenly she stopped and laughed as she thought, "It's just spaghetti!"

She shared her revelation with the other staff members. They laughed, too, and from then on, all they had to do was to look at each other and say, "It's just spaghetti!"

What in your life is "just spaghetti?" Even if you can't change it, maybe you can laugh at it. Speaking of spaghetti (which usually has garlic in it); I like what I heard Dennis Prager say, "A bad mood is like bad breath." ☺

A Shift in Consciousness

We each have a set of beliefs otherwise known as belief systems. It is from these beliefs that we approach and live our lives. **We get the outcomes that we believe we will**. Psychologists call this "self-fulfilling prophecy." Self-fulfilling prophecies work for both good and bad.

Our attitudes come from our belief systems. Our belief systems are the way we think; they are what our subconscious comes to accept as true. They become our reality and dictate how we live our lives. What we think we are, and what we think we can do, are direct results of our belief systems. These beliefs determine our expectations, whether for good or otherwise.

As I said before, **the good news is we can change our beliefs**. Affirmations, or, as I call them, Positive Expectation Statements™, are one way of accomplishing this. Repeating a word or a statement will probably not change the world, however **repeated often enough Positive Expectation Statements™ can change our thinking, our belief systems and therefore, our perspective so that we will get positive outcomes in our lives.**

My friend, Leilani Gowadi, said, "A miracle is a shift in consciousness." We can shift our positive expectancy by focusing on this statement, "This, too, in time, will pass."

Belief in the future is truly powerful. Positive expectancy influences our attitude greatly. Lives have been saved because people had positive expectancy. People who live with positive expectancy are just generally happier people.

Attitude determines whether we are happy or not. No matter what the circumstances, we can remain hopeful, if we choose to.

Hopeful people are optimistic and believe bad things are temporary and changeable. They have been found to be less vulnerable to depression, achieve more and have better health. Erich Fromm's theory is that violence is a result of hopelessness. He stated, "Psychologically speaking, destructiveness is the alternative to hope."

How we handle stress, and how it, therefore, handles us, depends upon our attitude. **Optimists are able to cope more effectively with stress**. As we noted, optimists have much less chance of developing stress-related illness and tend to recover more quickly.

Scientists have discovered that **worry, negativity and stress cause our brains to produce chemicals that can harm our bodies**. Stress also allows more free radicals to attack our systems, speeding up our aging process and increasing our chances of disease.

Again I share what the great philosopher, William James said, **"The greatest discovery of my generation is that a human being can alter his life by altering his attitude."** Knowing we always have options and choices, we can choose a new attitude.

My mother said it incredibly well; **"We give power to people and circumstances when actually the power is in our own mind!"** Steve Allen put it well also, "One of the nice things about problems is that a good many of them do not exist except in our imaginations."

Eleanor Roosevelt is noted for the profound statement, "No one can make you feel inferior without your consent." According to Dr. Martin Seligman, "Depression is a result of a belief in one's own helplessness." Mildred Barthel pointed out that, "Happiness is a conscious choice, not an automatic response."

We Get What We Expect

The simple truth is **we get just exactly what we expect in life**. We get what we believe! Not what we want, not what we hope for, not even what we affirm, just what we expect. **It is what we believe we will get that we get**.

True Life Example: My family was poor so I ought not to have expected that I could go to college. However, my mother always told me that I would go to college. Therefore, I had an expectation of my future that included college. I expected to go to college and so I did.

With the "belief" that I was going to college I studied diligently and applied myself to college preparatory courses earning scholarship funds along with a grant and student loans. It never occurred to me that I might not be able to go to college. Thanks, Mom.

A friend shared with me how different her expectations had been. Growing up she believed her only option was secretarial school or something similar. Even though she was intelligent enough to have gone to college that idea never occurred to her.

True Life Example: Here's another story about enjoying the results of positive expectation. I had been married and unemployed for a couple of years when I needed to get a job. I began interviewing and my friends were astonished when I was offered 9 out of 10 positions. Of course, I was; I had expected to, you see. I believed I would be good at all of the jobs. Aristotle said, "**What you expect, that you shall find.**"

We get what we feel we deserve. Robert Anthony expressed, "Your expectations of today will be your life of tomorrow." He also said, "Expectations control your life, so it is imperative that you control your expectations. If you expect the best, the best you shall have. However, if you expect the worst to happen, be assured that it will. By permitting your life to be dominated by negative thought patterns, you form the habit of expecting negative results. Studies show that ninety percent of people have negative expectations." As we previously discussed, these negative expectations are often referred to as limiting beliefs.

True Life Example: The following story is an example of how our expectations affect our outcomes. I enjoy a strong, deep massage. A massage from someone with a lighter touch tends to tense me even more and I don't get the benefit of relaxation. One massage therapist approached me with such confidence that I immediately relaxed, expecting a good quality deep massage. The truth is that she really had a rather light touch. Yet, because I had relaxed in anticipation, I got a better massage than I would have ordinarily.

True Life Example: I once wrote a poem for a boyfriend about him being a "free bird that I was not trying to catch, but just wanted to enjoy the flight with toward the sun." He told me that every time he had thought about leaving I had let him go, and so he had no reason to leave.

A few months later I became fearful of losing him – and so I did. In fact, I lost him within two weeks of allowing that fear of loss to take hold. Ah, the power of expectation!

So why don't people just change their beliefs? They don't recognize that the beliefs they hold are limiting and preventing them from getting what they want in life. They also may not be allowing enough time for change to become effective.

If you have areas in your life that need improvement, you probably have made a limiting decision. We usually form these beliefs when we are children. Once we can identify a decision we made that created a limiting belief, we can choose to change it and get what we really want in life!

It's important to pay attention to what you say to yourself. If you hear negatives ask yourself, "What's a more positive way of thinking about this?" A saying attributed to a Jewish king is, "Don't ever wish anything bad upon yourself."

Former First Lady Rosalyn Carter encouraged us, "If you doubt you can accomplish something, then you can't accomplish it. You have to have confidence in your ability, and then be tough enough to follow through."

U.S. Tennis Champion Venus Williams voiced, "Some people say I have attitude – maybe I do. But I think you have to. You have to **believe in yourself when no one else does - that makes you a winner right there.**" *[Emphasis Added.]*

Have Positive Expectations for Others, Too

Expectations of others can also affect their performance. How about the teacher that expects a child to be disruptive and a less than perfect student? The child will probably fulfill that expectation. How about the boss that expects poor results; he usually gets poor results, doesn't he?

We affect positive outcomes of others by our expectation. By responding to others on a positive "as if" basis we create a favorable emotional climate.

True Life Example: The movie *STAND AND DELIVER* is based on a true story about a dedicated math teacher, Jaime Escalante, who inspires his high school math class of dropout-prone students to learn calculus. He accomplishes this by building up their self-esteem. Ends up, they did so well they were accused of cheating.

True Life Example: I once worked at a large law firm as a "temp" (temporary Secretary). I had worked for many of the attorneys at the firm and had been there many months when the Head of Secretarial Services asked how I would feel about working for the Senior Managing Partner. "He has a reputation for being difficult," she said. "I know you get along really well with almost everyone and I really have no one else to fill this spot this week. Will you be willing to give it a try?'" I replied, "Of course." Little did she know that I saw this as a chance to prove my theory of positive expectancy.

Months later, I was still working for him and his reputation had changed dramatically. You see, I started a "goodwill campaign" for him. Everyone has good points if we just look for them. I look for them and, consequently, always find something good. His permanent Secretary said, "First she (meaning me) sold herself on his good points, and then she sold the rest of us!"

What is especially powerful about this is that I helped others to see his good points, others began to "expect" him to be nice and he met their expectations. His Secretary told me that other people were amazed at how nice he was to her. She expected him to be nice (I told her he would be, you see) and so, he was! She had "positive expectancy."

We Always Have Choices

Events and circumstances have power over us only if we allow them to. It's our **choice** if we stay angry or sad. We can change our attitude. We may not be able to change the circumstance but we can always change our attitude about it.

It is not our problems that get us down – it is how we view them. It is our decision what we allow. We have no control over other people, however we do control the effect their attitudes or opinions have on us. We have control over our perspective and how we see things.

Remembering we have choices and options, we have power. If we "choose" something, we are in control. If we let things happen to us, we aren't in control. Or, so it seems. Actually, we are always making choices.

Even, not choosing is a choice. We believe we "have" to go to work, but actually, we **"choose"** to go to work. It would be better to say, "I **'want'** to go to work." Choosing a different word may seem trivial; however, it reflects our attitude. It is more effective and satisfying to say we "choose to."

James Allen said, "They themselves are makers of themselves by virtue of the thoughts which they choose and encourage; that mind is the master weaver, both of the inner garment of character, and the outer garment of circumstance, and that, as they may have hitherto woven in ignorance and pain they may now weave in enlightenment and happiness."

Mr. Allen also shared, "The aphorism, 'As a man thinketh in his heart, so is he', not only embraces the whole of a man's being, but is so comprehensive as to reach out to every condition and circumstance of his life. **A man is literally what he thinks**, his character being the complete sum of all his thoughts."

Our Perceptions Are Totally Our Own

Absolutely no one shares our perception or views life exactly as we do. We each see the world uniquely. It is our choice how we see life. How do you see life? Do you see the rain? Or, do you see the chance for things to grow? Do you see a windy day? Or, do you see a chance to fly a kite? Do you see obstacles or opportunities? Do you see a half-full or a half-empty glass? The content of the glass don't change, however our attitude can.

When I say, "With my luck" I have learned to attach a positive expectancy to it.

I find that most people tend to focus on the negative aspects of an event. Ask yourself, "What is the worst thing that can happen? And, what's the worst thing about that? And, what's the worst thing about that?" This usually shrinks the matter from a mountain to a molehill in your mind.

Another approach is to ask, "What is the truth about this situation? What can I do to make it better?" It is up to us how we see things and how we respond. Shift your perspective by taking a step back.

By distancing ourselves, things become less important. **Someone described the human mind as a magnifying glass that exaggerates things.** Whatever you think the challenge may be it is probably not as bad as you imagine. Develop a positive attitude by reframing your perspective.

True Life Example: An injured friend called me, frightened about a terrible infection that had started to develop in her leg. In my effort to calm her, I said, "Okay take a deep breath. What's the worst thing that can happen?" She told me the doctors had said she might develop gangrene in her leg. "So," I continued, "What's the worst thing about that?" "They might have to amputate my leg," she fearfully replied. "And, what's the worst thing about that?" I asked. I continued until we had exhausted all the "worst" that could happen.

One might think this was cruel of me, yet I am very sympathetic, and always feel genuine concern. **What I believe, however, is that when we look our fears in the face and examine what is the worst thing that can happen we get back to the present where there is hope for the future.**

In the case of my friend, it took her out of gross speculation back to focusing on positive intent and maybe even bolstered her courage. I just reminded her that sometimes worry and fear are as painful as the "worst thing that can happen," and what a waste when the best can happen as easily as the worst.

Asking, "What's the worst thing that can happen?" simply reminds us to look at the big picture. Even if the worst thing does happen, becoming sick with fear and worry will not change the outcome.

It would be better for us to take that same nervous energy and focus it on the vision of wholeness. Since some solutions are out of our control, it's always best to face "imagined" fears "head on."

So, what happened with my friend? Did she get gangrene and lose her leg? No! The infection cleared up and she lived to run for miles!

"What's the worst that can happen" is not about dwelling on the negative or making up scary scenarios. It is more like that flight attendant, with the fear of deep water, who faced the most frightening swimming test ever. The best course of action is to face the fear, take a deep breath, jump into the water, and kick like crazy until you reach the other side!

I would never minimize the tragedy that visits the lives of some people, and none of us know how we will handle bad things that can happen to us, until they do. It simply does no good to dwell on them beforehand.

To stay positive in the moment can fortify us and sometimes precedes great miracles we never could have imagined. To live in dread is to be one of the "walking dead."

If the worst does happen, no matter what that might be, it will serve us better to take our creative energy into the next level of positive results. Miracles happen, more often than not, with prayers and meditations for a positive outcome. **It's also wise to ask, "What's the best thing that can happen?"**

I'll Be Happy When

Often we go through life living for tomorrow and for some future event or set of circumstances. We convince ourselves that things will be better when this, that or the other thing happens.

Marshall Goldsmith shared, "The great Western disease is, 'I'll be happy when. When I get the money. When I get a BMW. When I get this job.' Well, the reality is, you never get to when. The only way to find happiness is to understand that happiness is not out there. It's in here. And happiness is not next week. It's now."

Don't postpone your happiness. There is no better time to be happy than now. We will always have creative challenges of one kind or another. Why not just decide to be happy now anyway?

Many times "What if" begins a negative sentence. "What if I can't get there on time?" "What if I don't get the job?" "What if he doesn't like me?" These anxious thoughts are projections into the future – not reality.

Stop with the "what ifs." They just waste your energy and time, just like "should" and "when." Here again asking, "What is the worst thing that can happen?" will help stop those "What ifs." You can also use those words to expand your mind by asking, "What's the best thing that might happen?"

Mistaken Certainties

Expectation focuses on the future. **Use expectation positively**. An expectation of bad things is an act of fear. Fear is perceived; fear is an attitude. Since we can change our attitude, we can choose to release our fear.

It is my firm belief that the main thing, if not the only thing, that truly limits us in life is FEAR. Without fear, we experience peace and happiness.

Things are not always as they may seem. We often perceive a situation as negative when it is, in fact, not. We allow current situations to cloud our belief – which causes us to have what Dr. Robert Anthony, calls "mistaken certainties." Ponder that idea for a minute.

FEAR is an attitude – and, as I said, because we can change our attitude, we can change our fear. One of the best ways to do this is to experience the fear and do it anyway! Then we are no longer afraid. We can also face the fear and look at our beliefs about it and change those beliefs and, therefore, change the fear.

NO FAIRY GODMOTHER REQUIRED

Many people are afraid of the unknown. Yet the unknown also holds all of our potential good. Instead of being fearful, embrace life and its opportunities. It is possible to conquer fear.

Usually, just facing our fear will shrink it. Our imaginations are powerful tools. We can use them to help us, not hinder us. Rhonda Britten said, "Whether you know it or not, fear has developed your likes and dislikes, picked your friends, and raised your children."

Fear can affect every aspect of our lives. Learn to release fear and get on with our lives and being happy.

Dr. Paul Hartunian, famous publicity expert and a licensed medical doctor, claims that we are born with only two real fears. These two fears are loud noises and the fear of falling.

Dr. Hartunian said, "You lose those early on. You create any other fears. They aren't real." When asked how to stop these created fears he said, "Stop it. Just stop it. Say you have a fear of bridges. If I put one million dollars in cash on the other side and said, you could have it if you walked across the bridge, nude, in front of a crowd of people, you'd do it. Why? The reward is greater than the pain. Make the rewards greater and the fears will vanish."

It's appropriate here to reiterate Brian Tracy's quote, "The key to success is to focus our conscious mind on things we desire not things we fear."

The powerful information here is that fear is learned. If we learned fear, we can unlearn it. How? By being aware of this truth and refusing to accept it any longer. Recognizing a negative behavior is one of the first steps to getting rid of it. Next time fear rears its' ugly head look it in the face. Acknowledge that it is probably not real. This will begin the change to freedom and trust.

Embrace the concept of "feel the fear and do it anyway." Yet, also honor your instincts when your protective voice inside shouts, "Stop! There is danger here!"

How to Overcome Fear

1. **Determine if the fear is justified.** Sometimes it is. If we are facing possible bodily harm, it is justified. If someone is holding a gun to our head, it is justified. If we have a fear of a friend betraying us and that friend has, in fact, betrayed us before; that may be justified. However, most of the time, fear is not justified; it is not real. FEAR = False Evidence Appearing Real.
2. **Face that fear by taking action**. Even a small step will energize us and help keep us from becoming immobilized.
3. **Affirm your power over the situation**. We can remind ourselves of our courage and our abilities to handle challenges.

Act As-If

Live as if you are already the person you want to be or already have what you want. You have heard the expressions "act as if" or "fake it until you make it."

The truth is what we think about expands. We attract more of what we already see in our life; what we project out, we attract and forms our expectations.

Keep Your Eye on the Benefit

Concentrate on the benefits instead of the features and you can "sell" yourself on an idea. In sales, they teach you to "sell the benefits, not the features." Let's discuss how features and benefits are different. Then we can focus on the benefits, which will motivate us to accomplish our aim.

A feature is something that describes something. It is part of something. For instance, you might refer to the features of your car. It has got an automatic transmission, a four-cylinder engine, is painted blue, etc. Those are features.

A benefit is something you enjoy while owning that feature. It's the outcome or the result of use. For instance, an automatic transmission is easier to drive and therefore less tiresome than a standard transmission. Benefits motivate us. They are the reason we do things. We can motivate our self by creating and using benefit statements.

What is a benefit statement? Here's an example using eating healthier. Eating broccoli and spinach would be *features* of becoming healthier. The *benefits* would be more energy, losing weight, or clearer skin – outcomes of eating better.

Benefits are the result we can expect from a change in our behavior. We don't start a diet because the food is healthier (that's a feature). We start a diet because we want the benefit we will get. So, sell yourself on the benefits.

Prosperity is an Attitude

True prosperity is not necessarily about financial success, possessions or security. It's an attitude. It's recognition of what is enough for us. When we have enough we are satisfied and happy. I'm convinced that being happy actually attracts even more good and ultimately multiplies our happiness in life.

Catherine Ponder in her book, *THE DYNAMIC LAWS OF PROSPERITY*, refers to "prospering." She said that we are prosperous to the degree that we are experiencing peace, health, and plenty in our world.

She further said that while prosperous thinking means many things to people, it gives us the power to make our dreams come true, whether those dreams are concerned with better health, increased financial success, a happier personal life, more education, travel, or a deeper spiritual life. In other words, she agreed that if you are happy you are prosperous.

I also like how Terry Cole-Whittaker described prosperity. She said, "To prosper is to experience sufficiency and satisfaction regardless of where you are, what you are doing or what you have."

Connierae Andreas and Tamara Andreas described "prosperity" beautifully, "Some of the experiences people experience when functioning from the Core Self include: wholeness, inner peace, well-being, love, aliveness, being fully grounded and centered within your body, fully aware of your body and emotions, a clear perception of the world, behavior that is in alignment of your values, easily acting in your own best interests, a positive sense of self, an awareness of who you are, resourceful with a sense of choice of how you feel and what you do. These are general attributes, individuals will naturally experience variations."

Charles Spurgeon expressed, "It is not how much we have, but how much we enjoy that makes happiness." An unknown author said, "A rich person is someone who has more than enough." If we believe we have more than enough than we do!

Youth is an Attitude

Americans seem preoccupied with the fear of aging. How old we *appear* is often a reflection of the attitude we project. An unknown author said, **"Maturing means reacquiring the seriousness one had as a child at play."** As Marcia Gay Harden put it, "Ninety percent of how you look is how you feel about yourself."

True Life Example: Many Japanese love the essay, *YOUTH* by Samuel Ullman. Several hundred top businesspersons and government leaders gather in Tokyo and Osaka to celebrate their unending admiration of Ullman's essay. Konosuke Matsushita, founder of the Panasonic Company, said that *YOUTH* has been his motto for more than 20 years.

Read the following essay and I bet you will agree that this is a powerful essay for a man who began writing in his 70s.

YOUTH

Youth is not a time of life; it is a state of mind; it is not a matter of rosy cheeks, red lips and supple knees; it is a matter of the will, a quality of the imagination, a vigor of the emotions; it is the freshness of the deep springs of life.

Youth means a temperamental predominance of courage over timidity of the appetite, for adventure over the love of ease. This often exists in a man of 60 more than a boy of 20. Nobody grows old merely by number of years. We grow old by deserting our ideals.

Years may wrinkle the skin, but to give up enthusiasm wrinkles the soul. Worry, fear, and self-distrust bows the heart and turns the spirit back to dust.

NO FAIRY GODMOTHER REQUIRED

Whether 60 or 16, there is in every human being's heart the lure of wonder, the unfailing childlike appetite of what's next and the joy of the game of living. In the center of your heart there is a wireless station: so long as it receives messages of beauty, hope, cheer, courage and power from men and from the Infinite, so long are you young.

When the aerials are down, and your spirit is covered with snows of cynicism and the ice of pessimism, then you are gown old, even at 20, but as long as your aerials are up, to catch waves of optimism, there is hope you may die young at 80.

I Expect Miracles

Small events can be more important than big ones. Life is made up of innumerable small events that unfold minute-by-minute, hour-by-hour, and day-by-day.

Count your blessings, keep your attitude positive and live with positive expectancy as Dr. Wayne Dyer does. He said, "I am realistic – I expect miracles."

I do, too. I have had so many "miracles" in my life the last couple of years that I now expect them; and so they keep showing up. Thank you, God!

One of my miracles was winning Tom Antion's $5000 Internet Marketing Buttcamp. ☺ (Yes, that really is the name of his workshop.) Then there was the free ticket worth $497 to an empowerment summit.

Free rent by house sitting for nine months while I was writing this book was really a special blessing, and that came to me. It was not something I had searched out.

You may say I was just lucky. There have been too many things for me to call them luck!

How about sitting next to an attorney who specializes in copyright one night at a restaurant, at the time I was about to research using quotes. "Coincidence?" you might ask, and I'd answer, "Yes, the coincidence of another 'miracle'."

So, decide today to start seeing the miracles in your life. You can think yourself happy! Utilize the Happiness Action Tool™ of perspective to live your happiest life!

Positive Expectation Statement™

For Happiness Action Tool™ #6
THE POWER OF PERSPECITVE

"I approach life with positive expectancy."
(6 words)

For free gifts to support you in being your happiest, visit your happiness community at TheHappinessCommunity.com.

CHAPTER NINE

Draw a Mental Circle of Love

HAPPINESS ACTION TOOL™ #7

The Potency of Acceptance

"To love one's self is the beginning of a life-long romance."
~ Oscar Wilde

"We cannot change anything until we accept it."
~ Carl Jung

"A man cannot be comfortable without his own approval."
~ Mark Twain

The following poem by Edwin Markham was my mother's favorite poem. She quoted it many, many times, as I was growing up. It reflects the concept of acceptance well.

"He drew a circle that shut me out,
Heretic, rebel a thing to flout,
But love and I had the wit to win,
We drew a circle that took him in."

Since her death, I am even more conscious of that poem, and the profundity of my mother for holding it so dear. She epitomized the poem, always drawing her circle larger, warmly accepting everyone. It really works to draw that mental circle. I suggest you try it. It can be quite astonishing.

Unhappiness is often from lack of self-esteem that shows up as anger. When you see someone who is unhappy and/or angry at life, draw a mental circle of love around him or her. Recognize that he or she is in pain and mentally envelop them with love and kindness. It's wonderful to see people respond positively, as they soften and drop at least some of the anger. By drawing them into our space of peace, we can often change their mood. Everyone needs recognition and to feel validated. There is a wonderful YouTube video called

VALIDATION. You can see it at your club website, TheHappinessCommunity.com.

Some people think of acceptance as resignation. I do not agree. Resignation means we give up. Acceptance means we relax into that reality of something.

This doesn't mean we don't fix what we can. Will Garcia said, "The first step toward change is acceptance. Once you accept yourself, you open the door to change. That's all you have to do. Change is not something you do, it's something you allow."

Acceptance is the easier thing to do. It is less effort to relax and let things be what they will. Resistance is hard work. This is where my THEORY OF THREE comes into place. If we cannot change a condition and we can't or will not move away from the negative situation, then accepting it is the only alternative.

Suzanne Matthew explained it like this, "I spend most of my years trying to control things, but I've come to realize that perfection is a self-defeating goal. I can now embrace life with all its imperfections and it makes my day easier - a lot more fun. This is one of the most valuable lessons my love for my children has taught me." George Will said, "The pursuit of perfect often impedes improvement."

Forgive the past. Look to the future. Forgiveness opens the door to acceptance. We cannot change the past. All we can do is accept what lesson it holds. This does not mean we resign ourselves and give up. It does mean we let go of the past and focus on the future.

Accept Yourself and Others

Johnny Depp shared, "If there's any message to my work, it is ultimately that it's OK to be different, that it's good to be different, that we should question ourselves before we pass judgment on someone who looks different, behaves different, talks different, is a different color."

Whether this applies to how you view you or someone else, these are powerful words. We must allow change in ourselves, as well as others. We can be so judgmental of ourselves, as well as others. William D. Brown explained it in saying, "Failure is an event, never a person." Virginia Satir shared, "Feelings of worth can flourish only in an atmosphere where individual differences are appreciated, mistakes are tolerated, communication is open, and rules are flexible – the kind of atmosphere that is found in a nurturing family."

I like this quote by Ruby Bayan-Gagelonia, "Learning to love yourself is the greatest love of all. Before you can love others, you must first love yourself."

You may think that other people have it "all together." Maybe you think that another student is succeeding at both his academic studies as well as excelling at sports, while you feel you are just getting by. What you may not know is that the other student may be suffering from incredible insecurity and maybe even considering suicide! You might think that another woman is raising perfect children, keeping a spotless house, and having a great career, yet you see yourself as just getting by. Do you really know what her life is like? Do you know if she is happy or if her marriage is happy?

When we can't meet all the expectations we have set up for ourselves we think there's something wrong with us. We probably have set our expectations too high and are not giving ourselves credit for what we have accomplished so far. Recognize and value yourself for what you do accomplish.

Instead of accepting the beauty in each of us being different, we make cruel remarks about others, and sometimes, even about ourselves. What a waste of a lot of precious time and energy.

Earl Nightingale shared, "The person who criticizes others all the time is, in reality, unhappy with oneself. He or she concentrates on what's wrong with everything instead of what's right with it. This person concentrates on the specks of dust that may be found on any masterpiece and, as a result, goes through life missing the beauty and the wonders of life."

If you owe someone an apology, show self-esteem, give it and look forward. If you feel someone owes you an apology and, yet, does not give it, for your own sake know that hanging onto resentment, grudges and hurts just builds calluses and scar tissue around your heart that impedes your ability to relax into your happiness.

Sometimes the things we see as intentional inflictions of pain are really misunderstandings, or reactions to misunderstandings. We can forgive and begin to heal the energy around the relationship by believing that in their best heart it was never their real intention to hurt us. Ultimately, the kindest thing for everyone involved, although it may take tremendous courage, is to forgive.

True Life Example: When I separated from my husband, I was very angry with him. After ending up in the hospital with stomach problems I had to find a way to release the negative emotions I was holding onto because they were hurting me, not him! I realized that there was more misunderstanding than the intent to hurt. I accepted his humanness and drew a circle that took him in. I also forgave myself for my humanness for feeling hurt and angry. We were able to come to a place of friendliness, which I will always be grateful for because he unexpectedly died shortly after that.

Accept other people's humanness NOW. Draw a mental circle and take in the whole world! I've found it helpful to picture the person I perceive has hurt me as being a child who has is just doing the best they can to get by, too.

Accept Your Feelings

A passage from *LOVE BLOCKS* by William P. Ryan and Mary Ellen Donovan impressed me, "... defenses work against self-esteem. To have a genuine sense of self-worth, an individual needs to say, 'I am a feeling being with a capacity for the whole range of human emotions – and that's okay.' Put another way; respecting yourself means respecting your feelings – all of them."

Please never tell yourself you "should" feel anything. Either you feel something or you don't. We discussed in a previous chapter how should is a useless word. Instead, accept your feeling, or as some might say, "own" them. Make your feelings your friend and figure out how to harness their power and utilize them beneficially, as guides perhaps to insights and solutions.

Often considered a negative emotion, anger is sometimes justified. If it is justified, there is no reason to feel guilty about it; maybe it's time to utilize my "Theory of Three" process. If it is not justified, then you might want to regain your composure and be thinking of an apology. Either way, it could be your beginning of release.

Let Go of Resentments

Let go of resentments. They are so destructive. They just drain you of your energy. Refocus yourself to what is right with your life instead of concentrating on the negativity.

True Life Example: One day I was meditating, trying to figure out a solution to a creative challenge in my life. I found myself imagining trying to get to the other side of a brick wall - a tall, thick, long, brick wall. I kept picturing myself running up and hitting that brick wall and, of course, falling down. I kept hitting that wall harder and harder trying to make a dent in it.

Finally, in my mind I saw that I had collapsed and was just lying there. Then in my mind's eye, I saw myself getting up, calmly approaching the brick wall, and finding a door that I could use to go to the other side. Now why did I tell you this story? Because it is symbolic of how we often try to figure things out and once we let go and stop fighting we suddenly, clearly, see a solution.

"Two Words"

Do you ever have "one of those days?" We all have. Even if it's just "one of those hours," or "one of those minutes," these times of things going wrong interfere with our life. The simple way to handle those times is what I call the TWO WORDS TOOL.

One of my ex-roommates and now a very good friend, Patty Roseman, and I used to look at each other at such times and we'd say, "Two words." This stood for one of my major philosophies in life, "This too, in time, will pass." "This too" is just two words, and why we didn't just say, "This, too" I'm not sure – but it made us laugh and got us through whatever frustration we were experiencing. Try "two words" to remind you "this too, in time, will pass," as it almost always does.

A story by an unknown author called *THE REAL MEANING OF PEACE*, illustrates how we can accept what is going on around us and still feel calm and good about our life. You can find the full version at TheHappinessCommunity.com. Please read it. It truly is beautiful and inspirational. It ends, "Peace does not mean to be in a place where there is no noise, trouble, or hard work. Peace means to be in the midst of all those things and still be calm in your heart. That is the real meaning of peace."

Self-Image is Learned

Self-worth is the direct reflection of self-image and, self-image is learned. Therefore, if self-image is learned, then we can come into recognition of our self-worth.

One feeling of self-worth breeds another. I love the way Mark Victor put it, "What you believe is what you achieve. You become what you affirm: positively affirm your greatness, genius and full potential."

Many people tend to compare themselves to fashion models and actors, narrowly focusing on outward appearances. The truth is it is our inner radiance and strength that shines through that attracts the admiration of others.

True Life Example: Walter Matthau charmed and delighted audiences for a lifetime with his not-so-handsome face. He did not climb to fame without personal challenges, two of which were "smoking and gambling." He made a decision to change his life after a heart attack in 1968 and never looked back.

True Life Example: In addition, I've heard stories that no one in Hollywood believed Danny DeVito would amount to anything, because agents could not believe there would be much work for a character that looked like him. For a few years, he was disillusioned with Hollywood. However, he believed in himself, and pursued and fine-tuned his trade, until the opportunities of his profession presented themselves and allowed him to be fruitful in his career.

The classic story, *BEAUTY AND THE BEAST*, has always been a favorite, symbolizing inner beauty. The modern day fairy tale, *SHREK*, applauds choosing the happy life of an ogre to one of perfection which some seem to see in only a physically beautiful prince or princess.

Since I believe self-esteem is important to our core prosperity and happiness, it seems important to point out a distinction. You see, **self-esteem is not a personality steeped in ego. Nor is a humble loving soul lacking in self-esteem. Self-esteem is a feeling of worthiness.** With self-esteem, you have the strength, clarity and focus to accomplish what you want in life.

How to Accept

1. **Recognize any resistance you may have.** Acceptance is being without resistance, which is not the same as feeling resigned to something. Acceptance is favorable reception of something. So first, recognize what you feel resistance to. Recognizing that resistance can help you identify what may need to change, or better yet, what you may want to accept.
2. **Analyze the resistance.** Is it the voice of fear appearing falsely, to protect us, to prevent us from taking a leap of faith, warning us that we may fail? It could be our ever-faithful intuitive guide telling us that something would be best if changed, instead of simply accepted. Could it just be our attitude that would be better if changed to acceptance?
3. **Look for the good.** See what good you might find in the situation and how this might benefit you.
4. **See the big picture**. Having identified the resistance you want to overcome, disarm it by embracing it mentally in a circle of love. Bless it. See all the good that can come from it, and release the rest.

Toot Your Own Horn

Many of us doubt ourselves because of the many things we heard as we were growing up. Things like, "Don't toot our own horn." We also may have heard crazy things about "getting a big head" if we were recognized for our accomplishments. Well, in my not so humble opinion, it would be a much nicer world if more of us had "bigger heads," if we got "bigger heads" by filling them with healthy thoughts of appreciation for our life, its opportunities and ourselves.

The word healthy is important here. I'm not suggesting that we have false images of our self-worth. I am saying that with healthy self-appreciation we are in charge of the quality of our choices. We will choose only healthy substances to put into or on our body, and we will be aware of what we allow in our mind. With a healthy self-appreciation, we become happily self-reliant, free to pursue the life we choose. Knowing we are responsible for all the choices we make we'll be inspired to make better choices, improving our life and the lives of those around us.

The importance of self-image as it relates to happiness is very powerful. A healthy self-image is what helps us nurture and enhance our core prosperity, and doing something progressively harder after each accomplishment, will increase our sense of self-worth. With our new enhanced confidence, we will release the fear that blocks us from our highest good.

Accept Your Worthiness

Accept your worthiness and your right to live your happiest life. We each deserve to be happy. Claim that right. Somerset Maugham said, **"It's a funny thing about life, if you refuse to accept anything but the best, you very often get it."**

Positive Expectation Statement™

For Happiness Action Tool™ #7
THE POTENCY OF ACCEPTANCE

"I fully accept everyone, including myself."

(6 words)

For free gifts to support you in being your happiest, visit your happiness community at TheHappinessCommunity.com.

CHAPTER TEN

Watch Out For the Boomerang

HAPPINESS ACTION TOOL™ #8

THE VALUE OF ACKNOWLEDGEMENT

"I make it a rule always to believe compliments implicitly for five minutes, and to simmer gently for twenty more."
~ Alice James

"Few things help an individual more than to place responsibility upon him, and to let him know you trust him."
~ Booker T. Washington

"Keep away from people who try to belittle your ambitions. Small people always do that, but the really great make you feel that you, too, can become great."
~ Mark Twain

We all need to feel special, to have the importance of our existence affirmed. We establish relationships to reaffirm this sense of identity and significance; to know we matter; and that we count in this life.

Relationships can be relaxed, warm and even easy. Maintaining a mutually satisfying relationship may require effort, yet it can be pleasant effort that will reap rewards far beyond the energy expended. A significant way to maintain a lasting relationship is utilize the Happiness Action Tool™ of acknowledgment.

Recognizing is Valuing

To acknowledge a person is recognize a person's uniqueness and show appreciation for them. Actor Celeste Holm told us, "We live by encouragement and die without it – slowly, sadly, and angrily." Napoleon Hill said, "The person who sows a single beautiful thought in the mind of another, renders the world a greater service than that rendered by all the fault finders combined." Mother Teresa shared with us, "Kind words can be short and easy, but their echoes are truly endless."

Goldie Hawn shared, "I have witnessed the softening of the hardest hearts by a simple smile." Yes, just with a simple smile. An unknown author said, "If you think you are too small to be effective, you have never been in bed with a mosquito."

The World Could Use More Big Heads

Most people believe it's *not* good to brag. They also believe it's best not to compliment a person too much because this breeds large egos and swelled heads. Well, I think the world could use more "big heads." I believe we need to value ourselves, as well as others, more and based on the findings of some serious studies, I am right.

Be sure to acknowledge yourself as well as others. Be your own best cheerleader and give yourself credit! "We ourselves feel that what we are doing is just a drop in the ocean," Mother Teresa shared, "but the ocean would be less because of the missing drop."

Feeling good about yourself, you are able to support others more effectively. Graciously accept acknowledgement from others. We can't give if we have nothing to give.

As Mark Twain said, "If you can't get a compliment any other way, pay yourself one." You might laugh at this, but I believe he meant it in all sincerity.

Roderick Thorp shared, "We have to learn to be our own best friend because we fall too easily into a trap of being our own worst enemy." Boogie Jack said it well, "Most important of all, don't forget self-love, which is one of the most important loves you can know!"

Have you noticed that everyone likes to be around happy people? If we are happy, we just naturally spread that happiness. An unknown author explained my contention here well: "Real giving comes from overflowing! If you're needy then you're greedy!"

Brian Tracy expressed, "The more credit you give away, the more will come back to you. The more you help others, the more they will want to help you."

Dorothy Corkville Briggs in *CELEBRATE YOUR SELF* said, "If you live with quiet, deep gladness about your person, you don't need outer trappings or constant strokes to reassure yourself that you are OK. Yet because you affirm your worth and value, you let in outer affirmation when it comes."

With a "full cupboard," we are in a better position to reach out and share. Jim Britt in his book *RINGS OF TRUTH* shared, "Instead of praying in desperation, pray in appreciation! Somewhere along the line, we got the impression that giving is the ultimate act of spirituality and, of course, it is a wonderful thing to do. However, without the ability to receive, we have nothing to give ..."

I believe **conceit only masks lack of true self-love**. Pat yourself on the back when you have accomplished something. Let others praise you. Let them know you would like their praise and admiration.

Oh my gosh, yes I am suggesting that if your friends don't automatically praise you for something you have accomplished that you ask them to! Good friends will be happy to share your success, no matter how small, if you give them a chance.

Speak Up for Yourself

It's okay to ask for what you want. How can someone know you want something if you don't tell him (or her)? Now I did not say you demand something. I also did not say to be manipulative. However, asking for what we want is a significant trait of confident people.

The reasons people don't ask for what they want in life include fear of disapproval, feeling guilty, fear of causing conflict or making someone angry with us, as well as being considered different and not fitting in. If you are asking for something that is appropriate for you and will not harm others, then go ahead and ask for it. Then, acknowledge yourself by giving yourself credit for asking!

Here are a few words of caution. As quoted at the beginning of this chapter, Mark Twain said, "Keep away from people who try to belittle your ambitions. Small people always do that, but the really great make you feel that you, too, can become great." Keep the people in your life who make you feel great and let go of the others.

Celebrate Accomplishment

Why is it that we focus more on what we need to do, rather than on what we've already accomplished? Why not make a list of what we've done and celebrate that?

It's a good practice to do something every day that you do well. This will bolster your confidence regularly. Some accomplishments are major, yet there are many minor ones every day that help us achieve those larger ones. Choose to see those daily minor accomplishments for what they are: accomplishments you can be proud of.

There is real power in a sense of accomplishment. It motivates us to continue the journey of success: for success is a journey, not a destination. Enjoy the ride every day. Celebrate and reward yourself for even simple accomplishments. Take credit for them.

When we feel good about ourselves, we more easily feel good about others and so acknowledging them comes more naturally and easily. Truly acknowledge yourself for your accomplishments! Say, "Hey, I did that! Good for me!"

Occasionally, for no particular reason, I open a bottle of champagne and prepare caviar (albeit the grocery store variety ☺) with all the fixings to enjoy – sometimes all by myself. Sometimes it's just beer and pizza. It's a mini-celebration. What am I celebrating? I am celebrating "ME." It could be for any number of things – an accomplishment or I could just be acknowledging myself for my uniqueness. It may sound silly, but it's a way for me to remind me that I'm worth it. **You are, too!**

Create your own celebration the way that feels good to the child within you – maybe have that ice cream sundae or piece of chocolate cake you've been craving. It's a reward for accomplishments and for just being you!

A simple way to acknowledge yourself every day is to check off the things you've completed on your "to do" list. Add the things you also accomplished that day that weren't already on the list and check them off, too, being sure to list even the smallest things: telephone calls, errands, an overdue chore or a random act of kindness. The small things count, too. Take a look at all your check marks and acknowledge yourself for your accomplishments. Then determine if the things left unchecked on the list need to go on tomorrow's list, or do they really need to be done at all?

Focusing on what we DID get done motivates us to do more. Jack Canfield shared a great idea about acknowledging our accomplishments. "When you accomplish a goal, don't cross it out. Instead, write 'victory' next to it and move on to the next one. This way, whenever you have a bad day, all you have to do is to review your victories to feel good about yourself." I think I'll start adding a V (for victory) to each of my accomplishments.

Expression of Love

An anecdote for *CAMPUS COMEDY*, one of the regular columns in *READERS DIGEST*, illustrated how important it is for us to hear nice things, especially from those that are important to us.

> Judith Lichtenfeld told how her son called one evening sounding terrible. "Ma," he said, "my nose is all stuffed, I ache all over, and I think I have a fever. What should I do?" "Drink plenty of fluids and rest as much as possible, but you're in your third year of medical school. You should know all this," she responded. "I do, Ma," he said, "but I wanted to hear it from you."

We assume people know how we feel so we don't put into words our love, our concern, and our affection. Yet, those closest to us need our love and very often, they need verbal reaffirmation of that love. Plato said it eloquently, "At the touch of love, everyone becomes a poet."

Neurolinguistic Programming (NLP) teaches there are differences in how people take in the outside world. Some people are verbal, some are kinesthetic (feeling) and some are visual. Often we are a combination of a couple of these with one being our lead form. Some people need to hear compliments while others need to see an expression of your affection. Others best receive overtures of love by feeling it. Figure out what your loved ones "love patterns" are and share your love in a way they will best receive it.

Still, the easiest form of acknowledgement is a sincere smile. **Smiles are universal**. William Arthur Ward said, "A warm smile is the most universal language of kindness."

True Life Example: I read a story in *READERS DIGEST* titled *ALL THE GOOD THINGS* condensed from *PROTEUS* by Helen P. Mrosla. It was a wonderful story about a math teacher who had her students compose a list of the positive things they saw in each other.

She then carefully copied each of the comments onto a sheet listing the good things for each student and gave the lists to each student. She could hear the surprised voices of the children who did not know that others thought so well of them.

The story goes on that many years later one of her students named Mark unfortunately died. At his funeral, Mark's parents sought out the teacher to share that Mark still had his list, which he carried in his pocket. It ended up that so did many of the other students who were now adults!

Do not assume that others know our good thoughts about them. Tell them! Tell them now!

Jeanne Moreau gives us another reason for expressing love. "Age does not protect you from love. But love, to some extent, protects you from age." That's a thought worth considering.

Say I Love You

It's especially good to express your love verbally. The three little words "I love you" are so potent!

I express those words often and not just to the significant other in my life. There are different types of love. I do love my family and my friends. I started openly expressing those three words and the response I have had is warm reception and appreciation. The best part is they now openly express that love back to me.

Those words have a musical ring to them that nothing else does. I dare you to start expressing your love more verbally. Watch out for the boomerang effect!

Acknowledge the Joys, Too

Yet, people also need us to acknowledge their joys, too. Most of us are good at offering sympathy for someone's sorrow. Share in their joy as well.

Philosopher Arthur Schopenhauer said, "Anyone can sympathize with another's sorrow, but to sympathize with another's joy is the attribute of an angel." Be an earthly angel. Recognize another's joy, share it and help them celebrate.

Dr. Denis Waitley in his book *SEEDS OF GREATNESS* shared the following wisdom: "One basic definition of love, as a verb, is 'to value.' Love should be a verb, not a noun or adverb. Love is an active emotion. It is not static."

He continued, "Love is one of the few experiences in life that we can best keep by giving it away. Love is the act of demonstrating value for and looking for the good in another person." He says that, "L is for Listening, O is for Overlook, V is for Voice and E is for Effort."

Show Your Trust

One of the best ways we can acknowledge someone is to respect their ability to handle things in their lives. As quoted at the beginning of this chapter, Booker T. Washington said, **"Few**

things help an individual more than to place responsibility upon him, and to let him know you trust him." (Parents take note!)

I Love Birthdays

I just love birthdays! I believe they are very important. This is the one day of the year that we are recognized simply for being born. It's our own personal holiday. It's a happiness holiday.

True Life Example: I have given myself birthday parties for years. The first time my mother was rather appalled – concerned that people might think they had to bring me a gift. I explained that was not the reason for the celebration but that if people wanted to bring me gifts I would graciously accept them (you see I know that people enjoying giving). I asked her, "Who else knows everyone I know?"

I also love the process of planning the party – the love I put into the details shows in the delighted eyes of my friends and loved ones. It's my birthday, yet by sharing the day with those I love, I add joy to their lives as well.

When is your special day? Maybe you want to get busy planning your party.

Compliments Are Worth Millions

A compliment takes but a second and yet can last a lifetime. Acknowledgement can be very simple and yet, very powerful.

True Life Example: One day I was with my brother and we stopped by his house to drop off some things. As he carried a rather heavy item into his garage, I complimented his strength. His roommates happened to be standing there and I overheard him say to them, "Being with Gayleen is really good for my self-esteem. One day with her and I feel good for a month."

I genuinely love my brother, David. Complimenting him comes easy for me. I just hadn't realized that I had given him that much validation that day; I was making no special effort. Yet my small effort had a big impact!

Often we powerfully affect others with a simple comment and/or action without even being aware of it. Can you imagine how powerful it might be if we put a more concentrated effort in it?

True Life Example: A few days later, I witnessed this in action again. Talking with my hairdresser, I noticed his sincere smile and commented on it. His response surprised me. "Thank you," he beamed, "That makes my day." My simple compliment made his day? Wow! We often affect people and don't even know it.

I make an effort to validate other people's specialness. I really believe everyone is special so **I look for that specialness in everyone.** My mother told me that we could find something nice about absolutely everyone.

She's right, you know. We just need to want to find that specialness. I believe this is a skill anyone can develop. I'm glad my mother taught me this skill. I grew up hearing her voice tell me not to say anything if I didn't have something nice to say. Hey, I love to talk! No wonder I became very good at finding nice things to say. ☺

Give Everyone You See Today a Compliment

Acknowledgement is simple. Just a word, a compliment, a note or a visit can change a person's day and sometimes even their life. Look for the specialness in everyone you meet or even think of. Make that small effort that can reap such tremendous rewards – and then tell them what you see!

Look at each person you come into contact with today (or maybe all this week). See what you might sincerely compliment them on – and do so! When you practice, looking for compliments to give you'll find them often. At first, it may be difficult to find something about someone to compliment. However if you concentrate on it you will find something.

Are they wearing something that is flattering, say the color or the style? Do they have a twinkle in their eye? Do they have a nice or sincere smile? Did they do something you can recognize them for accomplishing? Just remember you want these to be sincere compliments; an insincere compliment is usually suspect, and strangely, even when not detected, has very little effect.

Praise vs. Flattery

"Many know how to flatter; few understand how to give praise." So goes a Greek proverb. There is a difference – a very big and significant difference.

The biggest difference is in the effect from the intent. **When we offer phony, insincere words of flattery they rarely give the recipient a genuine good feeling, whereas, a few well-chosen words of praise can uplift a spirit and have an effect for years to come.** Be sincere when you are acknowledging someone. To "acknowledge" means to recognize – not make up something.

William Arthur Ward said, "Flatter me, and I may not believe you. Criticize me, and I may not like you. Ignore me, and I may not forgive you. Encourage me, and I will not forget you." Peggy Noonan shared, "Candor is a compliment; it implies equality. It's how true friends talk."

My mother's belief, remember, is that there is something about everyone that we can praise. It's simply a matter of caring enough to look. The *LOS ANGELES TIMES* had billboards that echo this. They said, "Everyone has a story to tell." Usually, a very interesting story.

There are many reasons we can find to praise someone, including his or her character traits, their behavior or the way they look. For instance, you might praise someone for his or her integrity. You might also notice how someone else cares for him or herself and compliment them for that.

Words of Encouragement

True Life Example: Dionisio Negrete, M.D. personally experienced the value of reassuring words, "Early in my medical career, when I was a resident, I had a severe allergic reaction to a medication I was given. At one point, I honestly thought I was going to die. I sought the help of a colleague that was working that day. He looked me over, placed his hand on my forehead, looked me in the eye and told me in a very calm, reassuring voice not to worry, that I was going to be just fine. That simple gesture along with the time he took and the concern he showed for my welfare went a long way in helping me feel better. I learned a very valuable lesson that day and I've never forgotten it. I try to share that same reassuring feeling and concern with my patients,"

Dr. Negrete knew the need to deal with the emotional as well as the physical distress of his patients. "There may be someone who looks sad or who appears to be having a bad day," he noted, "I'll call them in and we'll talk for a little bit. Then before they leave, I may give them a hug, too! You can see an improvement happen before your eyes. You help take some of the aloneness away; you let them know somebody cares, that there is somebody to listen to their concerns!"

Mark R. Littleton shared these words of wisdom, "Let me offer you ways to give true words of encouragement..." He went on to tell us that we need to be sincere and simple, be sensitive to the time and place, recall personal examples of struggle. He further said that encouragement is simple, as it can be, "just a word, an anecdote, a compliment, a pep talk, a visit." As he said, "Take a look around. Pick someone out. Then give him the best you've got. Today."

> Here's a hint. Don't start a sentence with the word "you." It tends to put people on the defensive. The same goes for the word "no." It seems like you have discounted anything they say. Better to say, "That's interesting ..." Then tell your story. They will feel validated, and certain that you were listening, and in turn be more interested in what you have to say.

Here's a fun way to acknowledge someone without them even knowing. Every time you shake hands with someone, visualize that there is a wish in the palm of your hand.

The Power of the Written Word

A simple note can be a very effective way to acknowledge someone. It's also excellent because the recipient gets to keep your words of sentiment to enjoy again and again. Ranjan Bakshi said, "What a wonderful thing is the mail, capable of conveying across continents a warm human handclasp."

How to Acknowledge Others

1. **Make eye contact**. Look directly at the person and into their eyes.
2. **Smile**. This is the universal language.
3. **Listen with your heart** and your mind.
4. **Be candid**. Candor gives the compliment of equality.
5. **Touch others** when possible. Touch makes a connection as nothing else can.

Fred Bauer shared, "In a world too often cold and unresponsive, such notes are springs of warmth and reassurance. We all need a boost from time to time, and a few lines of praise have been known to turn around a day, even a life."

He explained the drawback with phone calls is that they don't last. "A note attaches more importance to our well-wishing. It is a matter of record, and our words can be read more than once, savored and treasured." He went on to tell us what it takes "to write letters that lift spirits and warm hearts." He said, "It is only unselfish eyes and a willingness to express our appreciation."

He added, "The most successful practitioners include what I call the four 'S's' of note writing ..." He said they are sincere, usually short, specific and spontaneous. I've come to realize the best-spoken compliments also follow those same four "S's".

True Life Example: I was having dinner with my friend, John Rogan, and we discussed compliments. He commented that I compliment people freely and easily. However, he pointed out that compliments are much more effective if they are specific.

About a week later, I received a card from John that made me laugh aloud. On the front were two hippopotamus in the water. The inside of the card said, "You have the cutest little ears." John added, "Now, that is a specific compliment." Touché, John.

The value of handwritten letters is becoming outdated. Telephones, email, instant messages and texting have changed the way we "reach out and touch someone." The written word can have impact again, and again. Little else has the same thoughtfulness that a handwritten note conveys. Written letters can often reach people when our spoken words cannot. Even those who love you do not hear you sometimes. If you want to be heard from the heart (and thus understood), put it in writing.

I have letters from years ago. I keep them as if they are a treasure – and so they are to me. After my mother and grandmother died, I found letters from both of them in what I call my "memory box." What a joy. Rereading their letters, I felt as if they were right here with me again!

Write Yourself a Love Letter

True Life Example: I had a boss tell me that I was not doing that good a job. The truth was he wasn't able to pay me that week and was trying to take the heat off himself. I was downright indignant. How dare him! My anger really motivated me at this point and I took the action of calling a number of people to say I was available.

The best action I took that night was to write myself a love letter. Yes, I really did. I had accomplished a lot in a very short time. I decided to tell me how proud I was of me. I still have that letter and read it when I need a boost or to be reminds me of my personal power and worth. Maybe it's time to write yourself a love letter!

How to Write Yourself a Love Letter

This will be difficult for many people. Not only am I suggesting that we compliment ourselves, and that we do it often and profusely, I now am suggesting that we put it in writing!

1. **Put yourself in a loving space.** Have a nice dinner by yourself and perhaps even a glass of champagne. Light the candles in the room and put on some soft music.
2. **Tell yourself in writing how special you are** and how proud you are of yourself. List your positive characteristics and your successes.

Hear With Your Heart

Author and Psychiatrist M. Scott Peck shared these words, "The principal form that the work of love takes is attention. When we love another, we give him or her attention... By far the most common and important way in which we can exercise our attention is by listening."

Words, though they can be very powerful, are only one means of communication and are often diluted or misunderstood by an ear that only hears on a loveless level. Listening to (which is different from just hearing) someone is the highest compliment!

Effective listening means not offering your opinion until you have given the other person a chance to express their views completely. Much of the time, we really don't connect with each other when we talk. We think we are communicating with each other, however we're simply taking turns talking. Practice hearing with more than just your ears. Listen with your brain and your heart.

We can acknowledge people in many ways. Verbal compliments are only one way. Express your affection in different ways without using the specific words "I love you." Here are a couple of ideas to get your started: share a hug; give a gift; share your last bite of food; give your loved one a massage, or hear them.

Barbara Sher in her book, WISHCRAFT, expressed, "When you're in that state, suffering in silence is the worst thing you can do. You need the relief of complaining now most of all. And there's only one thing you need from whoever is listening to you: to be heard. Real listening – quiet, sympathetic, and totally attentive – is one of the rarest commodities in our society. And, if we can't cure another person's ills, we don't want to hear about them: And that's because we don't know that listening is enough."

Richard Moss M.D. shared, "The greatest gift you can give another is the purity of your attention." Andrew V. Mason, M.D shared, "Sainthood emerges when you can listen to someone's tale of woe and not respond with a description of your own."

True Life Example: **Attentive listening is the best compliment you can ever give anyone.** To show interest in a person by giving them your full, undivided attention, is an amazing gift. Alice, my second Mom, gave me this gift by listening unconditionally to me for hours. My blood mother loved me very much and I know she cared about what I did and what I thought, however she was busy working to single-handedly support four children so she truly just did not have the time to sit and listen. I know that she was very grateful to Alice for giving me such healing attention.

I encourage you to pay someone the gift of listening. You just might change their life, although you may not even know it, as Alice did for me.

Touching is Effective Acknowledgment

True Life Example: Reverend Bredholt established the clown ministry that is part of the Baptist Medical Center in Columbia, South Carolina. He expressed that touching is a very important aspect of the clown ministry. "We always make sure we touch the person physically before we leave," he said. "Many patients, especially those with cancer or AIDS, feel that people don't want to touch them. They believe they are untouchables. We never leave a room without giving a hug if it's at all possible, or if they're too weak for an embrace, we at least will hold their hand or stroke their arm. Touching is so important. We want them to know that someone cares about them and wants to ease their pain, whether it be physical or emotional."

Leo Buscaglia said, "Too often we underestimate the power of a touch, a smile, a kind word, a listening ear, an honest compliment, or the smallest act of caring, all of which have the potential to turn a life around."

There is real power in the simple act of touching. I'm sure we would have less crime in this world if there were more touching and hugging. It's one of the easiest forms of validation. A gentle touch on the hand or arm will magnify any compliment. Sometimes the touch itself is the compliment.

True Acknowledgement is Unconditional

It is natural for us to shower babies with unconditional love and acknowledgement no matter what they look like, or what they do. We love them! This is the best way for us to acknowledge anyone, even ourselves.

You are valuable just because you are you. There is a little poem that expresses this so well called, *XVXRY PERSON IS IMPORTANT*. You can find a copy at your club website, TheHappinessCommunity.com. Its message is that every person is important, and would be missed: just as the letter E on the keyboard would be missed.

We think we are just one person and no one will notice if we do not do our best. However, just like the E key on a keyboard, each, and every, person plays a role in this world. **Yes, you are a key person. Everyone is!** Know that who you are is more important than what you were! Accomplishments really enhance our self-esteem yet we are worthy just as we are, whether we accomplish anything or not.

Dr. Denis Waitley said, "Separate the performance from the performer. In communicating with others, always treat behavior and performance as being distinctly separate from the personhood or character of the individual you are trying to influence." Actor Billy Bob Thornton shared, "If you love somebody let them know every day." I agree with that statement, whether **the** "somebody" is you or someone else!

Practice acknowledgement often – just watch out for the boomerang affect! With this Happiness Action Tool™, you will soon be acknowledging that you are living your happiest life.

Positive Expectation Statement™

For Happiness Action Tool™ #8
THE VALUE OF ACKNOWLEDGMENT

"I fully acknowledge everyone, including me!"

(6 words)

CHAPTER ELEVEN

Do It for You

HAPPINESS ACTION TOOL™ #9

THE BLESSING OF FORGIVENESS

"We read that we ought to forgive our enemies; but we do not read that we ought to forgive our friends."
~ Sir Francis Bacon

"Humanity is never so beautiful as when praying for forgiveness, or else forgiving another."
~ Jean Paul Richter

"The best gift we can give ourselves is to forgive - ourselves and others."
~ Gayleen Williams

Mary Lou Angelo in an article from *UNITY MAGAZINE*, explained how she came to understand the potency of forgiveness, "You know, everything you feel, say and do begins with a thought. If your thinking is negative, your life is negative. And there is no love in a negative life."

This comment was in answer to the author's question of how she could love herself. Her friend answered, "Write down the names of all the people you're angry with and have resentment toward and why. Then look at the resentments and see where you were wrong rather than wronged."

Ms. Angelo realized most of her resentments came from her own selfish desire for things to go her way. Some of the resentments she had held onto for years because they involved people who had wronged her seriously. She realized she had let her resentments become a part of her, "I had fed and nurtured and used them to excuse all my failures and inadequacies." Her friend suggested she forgive these people. She replied, "You've got to be kidding. I wasn't wrong in these cases. I can't forgive these people. They don't deserve forgiveness." Her friend said,

DO IT FOR YOU

"Ah, but you don't understand. Forgiveness is not for them. It's for you. Who are these resentments hurting?"

First, we decide to forgive. The next step in forgiveness is the most often missed; that of facing the situation with an open mind and heart. For, unless the injury is something as obvious as a vicious attack from a "would be" murderer or the like, very often **we may be holding to resentment or anger about someone or something that we don't even know the whole story about.**

Facing a person or a situation with a willingness to understand and forgive may put it in a different light that may diffuse all the potentially pent up stuff we have eating away at us. The person you have anger or resentment for may have "dealt the blow" based on a misunderstanding. Resentment is a human emotion. Just don't let the negativity take hold. Inventory your thinking and see what needs changing. Forgive yourself and refocus your thinking. **Often we focus anger at someone else, when we are actually angry with our self.** We don't want to accept our participation in the situation. Yet, when we do, it is much healthier. Besides, as an Italian proverb says, "To forget a wrong is the best revenge." ☺

Forgiveness is Critical to Our Health

Anger and resentment can actually make us ill. "Being able to forgive is critical to your health - even your physical health," shared Sidney B. Simon, Ed.D., Coauthor with his wife, Suzanne, of *FORGIVENESS: HOW TO MAKE PEACE WITH YOUR PAST AND GET ON WITH YOUR LIFE*. They said, "Suppressed feelings of resentment, hostility and victimization that go with a grudge – or the inability to forgive – reveal themselves in a number of ways... These include headaches, high blood pressure, insomnia and substance abuse." Glenn Clark expressed that, "If you wish to travel far and fast, travel light. Take off all your envies, jealousies, unforgiveness, selfishness, and fears."

Events and circumstances have power only if we allow them to. We choose to stay angry. Anger is not wrong – it's just a feeling, and feelings are not right or wrong. What we do about how we feel may be wrong. Choose to forgive. As discussed, forgiveness is a conscious choice and like most self-healing, is half the battle.

A key to forgiveness is being able to see the other person's perspective – to see "the big picture." We can let go of the past – not live in and hate it. Instead, chose to learn from it, and then turn it loose.

We Can Forgive the Person

True Life Example: When I separated from my husband lots of anger and blaming went on. I was very hurt and disappointed that it did not work out. I tried to hang on to what we had. However, he did some very unjust things to me and accused me of things that didn't make any sense. It was as if he had become a different person, one lacking the integrity, as well as the charm, that had originally attracted me. From my perspective, he was a man run amok. Still he was the man I had married and with the memory of loving him and the joys we had shared still fresh in my psyche, I wrestled with forgiving him. I sincerely made an effort to do so.

I finally decided that although **I could not accept his behavior, I could nevertheless forgive him as an imperfect human being. I could understand that he was more than his behavior.** As a human being, he was full of contradictions and imperfections, as we all are; some just worse than others. I realized that I might never understand his behavior, nor could I accept it, but I could understand that he was more than his behavior.

According to my THEORY OF THREE, if there is something we cannot change, then we either move away from it – or choose to accept it. I felt I had no other choice but to move away. It wasn't healthy for me to continue to have him in my life as a husband. There were too many memories that hurt, because either they made me sad for what was or what could have been, or they re-ignited the pain from the memory of his hurtful actions and the realization that reconciliation was not possible.

DO IT FOR YOU

> I need to add an important update here. My ex-husband died of congestive heart failure not long after I had forgiven him. I realize now he was literally "not in his right mind." Physical illness can cause us to have mental illness, as well. He had **not shared his health problems with me.** I am not even sure if he knew at the time he was ill. **I also see now that my anger at him from my confusion fueled the anger he returned to me**.

Sometimes we think we know what the truth is – or we guess at the truth – and we're not even close. I am so grateful we came to a place of peace before he died, and I know he, too, was grateful.

There is no question that some people sometimes do things that are malicious and with forethought. Murderers locked away in prisons are there to pay for their crimes and keep them away from the public. We do need a system of punishment; although a life without crime is a beautiful vision, it isn't very realistic. Yet, we can still see them as an imperfect human being and forgive the person, if not their behavior.

We can't change other people. However, we can choose how we react to our hurt feelings by focusing on something more productive. Maybe you can acknowledge something that was good about the person, or just be grateful for something positive in your life. Forgiveness is the best thing – for you! **At least forgive the person, if not the behavior**.

Lewis B. Smedes in *FORGIVE AND FORGET* said, "**Carrying a grudge is a loser's game. It is the ultimate frustration because it leaves you with more pain than you had in the first place.** Recall the pain of being wronged, the hurt of being stung, cheated, demeaned. Doesn't the memory of it fuel the fire of fury again? Do you feel that hurt each time your memory lights on the people who did you wrong? Your own memory becomes videotape within your soul that plays unending reruns of your old rendezvous with pain. Is this fair to you – this wretched feeling you have inside?"

He went on, "The only way to heal the pain that will not heal itself is to forgive the person who hurt you. Forgiving heals your memory as you change your memory's vision. **When you**

release the wrongdoer from the wrong, you cut a malignant tumor out of your inner life. You set a prisoner free – yourself." *[Emphasis added.]*

True forgiveness requires nothing in return and holds no conditions. We do this for us. We will feel much lighter.

We'll also feel better if we let go of guilt. Guilt is negative and, for the most part, non-productive and so accomplishes nothing good, except perhaps the desire to apologize and make amends for our behavior. It hurts **us**; so, let it go, for as Bernie S. Siegel put it, "When guilt rears its ugly head confront it, discuss it and let it go. The past is over. Forgive yourself and move on."

Blame Ends with Me

Arthur Freeman said, "... look at that word blame. It's an interesting coincidence that the last two letters spell the word me. Other people or unfortunate circumstances may have caused your pain, but you control whether you allow that pain to go on." He also shared, "Do not let the anger linger – it will eat away at you like a poison." Lynn Johnston old us, "An apology is the superglue of life. It can repair just about anything."

Layne and Paul Cutright expressed, "The sooner we can unburden ourselves of blame, the more effective we can be. Blaming others only entrenches us in the role of victim, removing us from our highest expression of personal power."

William H. Walton said, "To carry a grudge is like being stung to death by one bee." And, heard on *SATURDAY NIGHT LIVE*, "Don't hold a grudge, it's heavy, and it doesn't have a handle."☺

Paul Boese said, "Forgiveness does not change the past, but it does enlarge the future." We can't change the past. The past is the past. Forgiveness helps us create a better future. Forgiveness holds immense power because it mends separation moving us towards unity and love.

How do we forgive someone? As a first step, be willing to truly feel your anger and hurt. By honoring our feelings we are fully present which helps to release the feelings themselves. **People**

hurt others when they themselves are in pain. Recognizing the other person is suffering, our hearts can open in compassion. It is a fundamental part of the healing process. Billy Zeoli put it well by saying, "God has a big eraser." Have a big eraser, too! **The key to forgiveness is being able to see the other person's perspective.** There is usually more than one side to every situation. Stepping back and viewing the situation from the other person's perspective takes maturity, however the person who will benefit the most is you. Hatred and resentment (and getting even) can hurt us more than the other person.

How to Forgive

1. **Honor your feelings.**
2. **See the other person's perspective**
3. **Forgive the person, if not the behavior.**

Forgiveness is an Ongoing Process

Forgiveness is a life-long process. Unfortunately, we cannot forgive once and that will do it for life. We are human and we will feel negative emotions toward ourselves and/or others that will need forgiving at more than one point in our life.

Jerrold Mundis stated, "Forgiveness will never fail to free you." As Isabelle Holland said, "As long as you don't forgive, who and whatever it is will occupy rent-free space in your mind." Carrie Fisher said, "Resentment is like drinking poison and waiting for the other person to die." It's for sure that resentment robs us of energy. It also wastes time.

Use the Happiness Action Tool™ of forgiveness daily by forgiving yourself, as well as others. You'll see the blessing it brings in your getting and staying happy.

Positive Expectation Statement™

For Happiness Action Tool™ #9
THE BLESSING OF FORGIVENESS

"I fully forgive everyone, including me."

(6 words)

CHAPTER TWELVE

Count Blessings Not Sheep

HAPPINESS ACTION TOOL™ #10

THE MIRACLE OF GRATITUDE

*"Reflect upon your present blessings,
of which every man has many
– not on your past misfortunes,
of which all men have some."*
~ Charles Dickens

"I wept because I had no shoes, until I saw a man who had no feet."
~ Ancient Persian saying

"You can't be truly grateful without being happy."
~ Gayleen Williams

This is a very powerful quote from Melody Beattie, "Gratitude unlocks the fullness of life. It turns what we have into enough, and more. It turns denial into acceptance, chaos to order, confusion to clarity. It can turn a meal into a feast, a house into a home, a stranger into a friend. Gratitude makes sense of our past, brings peace for today, and creates a vision for tomorrow."

The definition of gratitude is "an appreciation of benefits received; it is being thankful." Many of us are familiar with the expression "a grateful heart." Gratitude is appreciating what we have in life. Brian Tracy told us, "Develop an attitude of gratitude, and give thanks for everything that happens to you, knowing that every step forward is a step toward achieving something bigger and better than your current situation."

Most of us have so much to be grateful for in our lives. Yet, we don't stop and acknowledge those blessings. Many of us are so much better off than most of the rest of the world. We have possessions and opportunities that some people can only imagine, or worse, that some could never even imagine.

When we slow down and practice being grateful our lives are so much happier. Looking through the window of gratitude, we see how good our lives are and can be in the future. Jim Carrey said, "I challenge anybody in their darkest moment to write what they're grateful for, even stupid little things like green grass or a friendly conversation with somebody on the elevator. You start to realize how rich you are." In a state of gratefulness, we are open to the flow of prosperity. We notice things we might not have. We see more joy in life. We see one flower and then suddenly there are many flowers.

Choose to look around and notice all the beauty there is around you. When was the last time you looked up at the sky and appreciated the beauty of the sun or moon, the clouds or stars? Plato told us that, "A grateful mind is a great mind which eventually attracts to itself great things."

According to Cicero, "Gratitude is not only the greatest of virtues, but the parent of all the others." When we focus on what is right in our life we are happier. Counting blessings in our life helps keep us clear about the value of our life. Noticing what is right in our life reminds us how much we have.

This doesn't mean we ignore the creative challenges in our lives. We just choose to focus on the positives instead; take action on the things we can and not worry about the rest. My THEORY OF THREE, tells us that we have three choices in life when presented with something we do not like? First is to change the situation, if we can. If we cannot, then we have two choices: to either move away from or accept the situation.

Doc Childre and Howard Martin shared these words, "You can never get to peace and inner security without first acknowledging all of the good things in your life. If you're forever wanting and longing for more without first appreciating things the way they are, you'll stay in discord." Naomi Williams expressed it simply and well, "It is impossible to feel grateful and depressed in the same moment."

Gratitude Heals

The state of gratefulness fills us with peace. From this place of peace, there is no anger and no hurt. Therefore, gratefulness is healing. **When you feel grateful, you cannot feel hateful**!

True Life Example: Do you ever have trouble falling asleep because of so many things on your mind? I have found an effective method to clear my mind for peaceful sleep. Start counting your blessings. I say start because I always fall asleep before I run out of blessings to count! For instance, I express gratitude for my warm, soft, comfortable bed, and the house that shelters me. I express gratitude for my material possessions and non-material possessions, such as my health and intelligence. I express gratitude, of course, for my loved ones, as well as the people in my life that are not so easy to get along with, because they remind me to appreciate the ones who are easy to get along with even more.☺ In addition, I express gratitude for the strangers who have come into my life and for whatever "learning gift" they have imparted. I express gratitude for food in my cupboards and the air I breathe, and a hug I received .... and zzzzzzzzzzz. Oh, excuse me; I fell asleep there for a minute. ☺ You get the idea. You can also bless everyone you can think of! These methods are more effective, and so much more rewarding, than counting sheep I've never met. ☺

You can discover a sense of wholeness as you appreciate the many blessings in your life. Dr. Denis Waitley expressed, "Happiness cannot be traveled to, owned, earned, worn or consumed. Happiness is the spiritual experience of living every minute with love, grace, and gratitude."

True Life Example: I attended a lovely party with a friend who was in quite a negative mood. Personally, I thought it was a great party. It was held at a beautiful home, decorated in a Hawaiian theme, with food appealingly served and delicious and a fully stocked bar offering anything you might want to drink, I felt grateful for my invitation to such a wonderful event. I was happy. That's the power of gratitude. **You can't be grateful without being happy!**

COUNT BLESSING NOT SHEEP

How to Be Grateful

Start a list of things you have to be thankful for and keep adding to it. You will be astonished at how long your list will get! Little things not only count, they can be precious discoveries that may make a difference. Here are a few ideas:

1. **Our health** and our ability to maintain it
2. **Our loved ones**, family and friends, each, and every, one
3. **Our accomplishments** AND recovery from mistakes
4. **Our pets**
5. **Our neighbors**
6. **Our personal treasures** and our right to choose them
7. **Our homes**, large or small, and the comfort they offer
8. **Our books** and other paths of entertainment and learning
9. **Our free ticket to enjoy the wonders of nature**
10. **Our job or career** and our plans for excellence
11. **Our surprise "miracles"** and acts of kindness from strangers
12. **Our opportunities to share** and be kind
13. **Our intelligence**
14. **Our moments of wisdom**
15. **Our energy** to "seize the day" and perhaps to dream
16. **Our freedom** to pursue happiness
17. **Our 21 Happiness Action Tools™!!!**

The list of things to be grateful for is endless; I challenge you to find as many as you can.

A state of gratitude is truly miraculous! William A. Ward asked, "God gave you a gift of 86,400 seconds today**.** Have you used one to say 'thank you?'" Only two little words, yet they carry so much weight. Count your blessings every day and you're sure to see the miracle of building your happiest life.

Positive Expectation Statement™

For Happiness Action Tool™ #10
THE MIRACLE OF GRATEFULNESS

"I find much to be grateful for everyday."

(8 words)

CHAPTER THIRHTEEN

Get a Helper's High

HAPPINESS ACTION TOOL™ #11

THE SPLENDOR OF GENEROSITY

"Help thy brother's boat across, and lo!
Thine own has reached the shore."
~ Hindu proverb

"Treat people as if they were what they ought to be
and you help them become what they are capable of being."
~ Johann Wolfgang von Goethe

"We make a living by what we get,
but we make a life by what we give."
~ Winston Churchill

Generosity is a Happiness Action Tool™ that gives to the giver and to the receiver. Vivian Greene expressed, "Giving is the highest expression of our power." Dr. Laura Schlessinger shared that, "You've touched people and know it. You've touched people and never may know it. Either way, no matter what your life feels like to you right now, you have something to give. It is in giving to one another that each one of our lives becomes meaningful." Charles Lamb told us, "The greatest pleasure I know is to do a good action by stealth, and to have it found out by accident."

Give What You Want to Get

Isaac Barrow shared that, "Generosity is in nothing more seen than in a candid estimation of other men's virtues and good qualities." What a good definition of kindness and generosity. One, almost guaranteed way, to be happier is to be generous. Sounds simplistic, however, it's as the *BIBLE* says, "Do unto others as you would have them do unto you." Peyton Conway Marsh expressed, "There is a wonderful mythical law of nature that the three things we crave most in life: happiness, freedom, and peace of mind – are always attracted by giving them to someone else."

A Helper's High

Case Study: **The more time spent in giving, the more happiness we feel.** The more happiness we feel the more we want to give. It's like a big beautiful circle. When we feel full, we are not just **willing** to give; we **want** to give! Walt Whitman saidl, "The habit of giving only enhances the desire to give."

Be aware you are liable to get a "helper's high."☺ You have undoubtedly heard of a "runner's high." Research shows that generosity creates a "helper's high." A Center for Health Sciences survey reported that **95% of volunteers experience this "helper's high,"** which is triggered by the release in the body of endorphins, those mood-elevating chemicals.

True Life Example: Friends tease me because I've don't even like wearing athletic shoes, much less jogging. I know what endorphins are, and so, I'm learning to appreciate walking more. Endorphins for me come while I'm doing something for someone else, like writing this book, knowing in my heart how helpful it will be. It gives me such a rush I want to jump up and shout! (Or, go for a walk.☺)

Since unconditional giving makes us feel good (and the more we give the better we feel), this ought to be reason in itself to be generous. However, it almost sounds like an oxymoron: being generous to get a selfish result. Yet, it does seem to be inevitable, that being generous makes the giver feel good. It follows that if you help others reach their goals, you will reach your goals sooner. The Dalai Lama told us, "If you want others to be happy, practice compassion. If you want to be happy, practice compassion." As Anne Frank said, "No one has ever become poor by giving."

Change the World through Generosity

William Wordsworth said, "The best portion of a good man's life - his little nameless, unremembered act of kindness and of love."

GET A HELPER'S HIGH

Margaret Mead shared, "Never believe that a few caring people can't change the world. For, indeed, that's all who ever have." We may think, "I'm just one person among so many, what effect could I have?" Perhaps a significant effect! History is full of stories of one person changing the world.

How to Be Generous

Simple Acts of Kindness ☺

Here are a few simple acts of kindness and/or generosity to give you ideas of ways to delight in being magnanimous!

1. **Find something redeemable** in the underdog.
2. **Visit a shut-in** and ask if you can run an errand for them.
3. **Do something for someone** less fortunate anonymously.
4. **Be patient and courteous** in traffic.
5. **Refrain from judgment or criticism** for a whole day.
6. **Feed a stranger's parking meter**.
7. **Hold the door open** for someone.
8. **Tip your server extra** for his or her service.
9. **Pay for someone else's meal anonymously**.
10. **Pick up something someone dropped** and return it.
11. **Volunteer for a worthy cause**.
12. **Bring home a thoughtful gift** (and maybe one for you).
13. **Pick up someone's trash** without anyone seeing you.
14. **Let someone go in front of you** in the checkout line.
15. **Compliment a stranger** with no expectation attached.
16. **Treat someone** to a small luxury.
17. **Smile**. ☺

Of course, there are many more... how many can you come up with? Share your creative ideas at your happiness club website, TheHappinessCommunity.com.

Be Generous to Yourself

Be generous to yourself. As we help others do not get lost in the shuffle. Focusing on others, we can neglect ourselves. We will do better helping others if we have lovingly taken care of ourselves first. How can we help others if we are depleted and sick? Allow yourself some guilt-free time. Set aside some time for yourself. Consider this an emotional investment – an investment in you! Helen Keller said, "When we do the best that we can, we never know what miracle will be wrought in our life, or in the life of another." **We can only do the best we can if we are the best we can be.**

It's good to give, and it is good to receive. How else can other people feel good about their giving? Ram Daas discusses this in many of his lectures and books. He explained we are encouraged to offer service to others, yet have trouble receiving the same service back from others. For instance, when we get sick we can view this as an opportunity to let others be of service to us.

True Life Example: Byron Morgan, 86 years old, was in a nursing home for several years after a stroke. He was a loving and vital man who was generous with his time, as well as his great ideas. I visited him often with his wife, Dell. He lit up at our arrival and we lit up at his joy in seeing us. I always marveled at his kindness, even with the challenge of his circumstances. Thinking of him still reminds me that love is a cycle – a circle of giving and receiving.

Dell told how Byron had to have about 10 blood tests one day. It was difficult to get blood from him and after the third technician had poked at him trying to find a vein, she found herself weeping in the corner because of his pain. Yet, once this technician finally got the blood, Dell heard Byron say, "Thank you doctor." Now that is generosity of spirit in the highest form. Ram Daas would have been proud of Byron. I know I was!

David R. Hawkins said, "Simple kindness to one's self and all that lives is the most powerful transformational force of all." Enjoy the splendor of the Happiness Action Tool™ of generosity as you build your happiest life to get happy and stay happy.

Positive Expectation Statement™

For the **Happiness Action Tool™ #11**
THE SPLENDOR OF GENEROSITY

"I now delight in giving and sharing."

(7 words)

CHAPTER FOURTEEN

Go With the Flow

HAPPINESS ACTION TOOL™ #12

THE SIGNIFICANCE OF TRUST

"There is wisdom of the head, and a wisdom of the heart."
~ Charles Dickens

*"In this world it is not what we take up,
but what we give up, that makes us rich."*
~ Henry Ward Beecher

*"The secret of health for both mind and body
is not to mourn for the past,
worry about the future, or anticipate troubles...
but to live in the present moment wisely and earnestly."*
~ Buddha

Trust releases fear. When we trust, we know that life will work for us; we trust that there is a process to life. As time goes on, we learn to trust more and more, releasing our fear. We look to the future with calm assurance and joyful anticipation. We become more aware of the blessings surrounding us in the present.

To me, trusting is "going with the flow of life." It is accepting that life works if we let it. It may not always appear so in the moment, however having belief in "the good," seems to bring about all sorts of unexpected, sometimes unexplained, support and benefits.

It's certainly a better choice than barraging ourselves with questions we may never find the answers for, trying to fix what we cannot fix, and having negative thoughts that attract negative conditions. It's my philosophy that, although I don't always know how, things have a tendency to work out if we trust they will.

GO WITH THE FLOW

I don't believe trust is a Pollyanna, free falling, detachment from responsibility. Like hope and faith, trust is one of the emotions that bridges the gap between our current challenges and dreams or visions, while we are realizing our solution. We can manifest trust most effectively by disarming false fears, getting out of our own way with our egotistically motivated control issues, letting go of resentment issues and fully allowing forgiveness.

This goes along with asking, "What's the worst thing that can happen?" If you believe that death is the worst that can happen, give your energy to making peace with life. Give your mind to positive thoughts of living, making all your choices in that direction. Don't fill up the "living moments" of your life with gloomy thoughts of dying. When you accept that death is inevitable you will do your best to prolong life, and just as well as importantly, be more conscientious in the enjoyment of it.

Don't Get Caught in Other People's Dreams

I firmly believe that we all know on a core level what is true and best for us. It shows up in our dreams and aspirations. Yet, often we choose to pay more attention to other people's opinions and judgments. Sometimes we even get caught up in THEIR dreams and sidestep our own. **We spend a lot of wasted time and energy second-guessing ourselves, or asking others their opinions, instead of listening to our own higher self,** instead of trusting ourselves and our connection to God, our higher self, higher consciousness, or whatever you call what I like to refer to as "The Divine It." Trust you are part of a master plan and that if you operate from integrity everything will be ultimately okay.

God always takes care of me. It's really quite remarkable. I do wish my creative self hadn't felt it had to keep proving this so many times. ☺ I have been at the point of losing everything many times and God always provides; sometimes at the very last minute, but He always does. I've started saying, "I have no need to worry. I have a rich and loving Father who always guides and cares for me." I find my life flows more easily now without so many "last minute" fixes.

This does not mean you sit back and just expect that things will work out. There is the expression that, "God helps those who help themselves." Do your best and let God take care of the rest.

***True Life Example*:** I once moved out of state only to find this was definitely not the right decision. I ended up "between homes," "between jobs" and uncertain of how I would get myself, and all of my belongings, back home. Well, not to worry; it all worked out. It always does. The mistake this time was in making a rash decision and not listening to my higher self at the start. I acted too quickly and didn't give myself a chance to check my head decision with my intuition or my higher self.

We can learn and benefit from our "mistakes," making us trust ourselves even more. Most of what happens in life is not a mistake. Some say, "There are no accidents." **Often what appears to be a mistake is a blessing in disguise.** Life is what it is; it's what we "believe it is." So, keep refining your beliefs so you enjoy better outcomes.

"Being" vs. "Becoming"

True Life Example: So often, we are so busy **becoming** that we forget to **be**, my mother pronounced one day during one of our conversations. It really caught my attention. I remember grabbing a pen and documenting her words, **"We're all so busy becoming, when all we need to do is be."** For years, those words, on that same scrap of paper, were on my desk as a constant reminder.

We often focus so hard on that goal out there that we are not here now. We are not present. **We truly only have NOW.** Life is for living and living is in the present. We can think about living in the future and remember living in the past; however, we can only live in the NOW. So, be here now. "Happiness," said Benjamin Franklin, "is produced not so much by great pieces of good fortune that seldom happen, as by little advantages that occur every day." So, live in the present. Savor the moment. Heed these words of the wise Eleanor Roosevelt, "Yesterday is history. Tomorrow is a mystery. Today is a gift. That's why they call it the present."

Take Time to Be Quiet and Calm

Take time to practice being still and quiet; both in your body and your mind. Only by becoming still, quiet and calm can we allow our intuition to come through. Being in a receptive state allows us to receive the guidance from those all-important gut feelings we otherwise tend to ignore.

Staying calm and trusting that there is a purpose to life allows us to experience life as it happens with greater clarity and therefore, handle life's challenges more effectively. **Worry comes from not trusting our capability to handle life's challenges.** When we expect perfection (a subjective abstract, at best) we tend to get overwhelmed by life's challenges.

On the other hand, if we trust ourselves to be able to handle life's challenges we have no need to worry or feel overwhelmed. Trust builds calm allowing us to hear guidance. Guidance shows us the way to better decisions, which gives us a sense of control and teaches us to trust – which builds calm. So, stay calm by trusting your own internal wisdom.

True Life Example: One of my best friends, Carol Latham, and I were talking about trust and expectations one afternoon. I happened to tape the conversation so I'll share some of it with you. "The first thing that comes to mind usually is instinctive and correct. Often times we second guess ourselves and we change it and then we end up with the wrong solution," Carol said. "Our first instinct is always correct," If we are going to trust ourselves then we trust ourselves, and that doesn't mean second guessing ourselves," I emphasized.

> A side note: Keep in mind that "second guessing" is not the same as thinking something through. Most times second-guessing is a form of procrastination or lack of commitment, showing our lack of confidence in ourselves.

"You know it's like we sometimes pray for something and we say, 'If it's Thy will I leave it in your hands'," Carol said. "Then five minutes later we say, 'Well, just in case, this is my second choice.' Or we pray for something six or seven or more times; rather than praying for it and letting it go knowing that if it is intended for us it will happen. We give it to God and then we take it back." I, added, "That comes back to what I was saying about expectations. When we can pray and expect to get something, we will get that or something better for us. We only keep praying because we don't expect to get it. We don't believe. We are not exhibiting our faith or our trust."

True Life Example: My mother called one day and asked me to pray about something. I said a quick prayer and went back to what I was doing. My mother called later and said, "Your prayers are so powerful." I felt guilty, because my prayer had been brief. After I hung up I realized that although it was brief I had **expected** my prayer would be answered in a loving way.

So, pray believing God loves you and wants you to be happy. Then, let go, trusting that your prayers ***will be*** **answered**. Eventually, you will realize all requests are answered, maybe not as you wanted, yet in an even better way.

A Totality of All Subconscious

While, this is not a book on religion and I am not here to sell you on the concept of any specific belief system, I want to share that I believe in a higher power, which I most often refer to as God. Emerson called it the universal mind and William James referred to it as the super-conscious mind. I think of it as being, "A totality of all subconscious." Others including my friend and co-author call it "Divine Love" and speak of Jesus. However we personally experience this part of our lives, it is definitely something bigger than any of us, and is something that we can tap into for love, wisdom and support.

I once described it like this: It is like there is a big mainframe computer and we are all mini computers. There are cords that connect the two. One cord, coming to the mainframe from the mini-computer, stays permanently connected so The Divine It (the mainframe) always knows what is happening with all the mini-computers (us). However, the other cord can be plugged, and unplugged, at will. Sometimes, due to negative thinking or because we think we have it all figured out, we choose to disconnect ourselves and not tune in. We choose to operate from our own limited resources, ignoring the treasure chest of infinite knowledge. The truth is we can tune in anytime and get any answer we ever need; yet we don't. How foolish is that?"

Remember Bobby McFerrin's popular song "*DON'T WORRY, BE HAPPY*?" The words in the song are truly words to live by. **The reality is that because we are always "in the now," our worry is always about the future, about something that has not yet happened - and may not happen at all!**

There is a simple solution to stress. Bless it; yes, bless the stress. It's said, "There is no growth without resistance." If you believe things happen for a reason, or at least believe you can learn from your experiences, your life will make more sense and it will be easier to trust that things work out for the best in the end. Remember it is only what we resist that persists! So, "don't worry, be happy!"

Regret is a Useless Emotion

One way to avoid the present is to regret the past. Regret, like guilt, is a useless emotion. I repeat: **Regret is a useless emotion.** Like guilt, regret has no purpose in being perpetuated or homesteaded. What good does regretting do? Does it change anything? No, it is burdensome and, oh so "wearing" on us! Truth is we have even less control over something that has already happened than we do about our futures.

Regret is a negative emotion that pulls us into the quicksand of negative thinking. **Doctors tell us that more than a few minutes of regret can turn into a psychosis**. It drains us of self-confidence and positive energy and steals NOW from us!

Instead of regretting something, use that time to forgive yourself. Then, make better choices for the future; choosing how you think today from a place of calmness and trust can very often heal the hurt from the past, and enhance the future.

In *LOVE IS LETTING GO OF FEAR*, Gerald G. Jampolsky, M.D. talked about how we replay the past superimposing memories onto the present, "The mind can be thought of as containing reels and reels of motion picture film about our past experiences. These images in our mind are superimposed on the end through which we experience the present, as well as on each other. Consequently, we are never really seeing or hearing it as it is; we are seeing fragments of the present through the tons of distorted old memories that we layer over it."

Dr. Jampolsky went on, "If we are willing, we can with increasing effectiveness use active imagination to wipe away everything from those old reels except Love. This requires letting go of old past attachments to guilt and fear... We often believe that the fears of the past can successfully predict the fears of the future. The results of this type of thinking are that we spend most of our time worrying about both the past and the future, creating a vicious circle of fear, which leaves little room for Love and joy in the present."

Fear Holds Us Back

Negative emotions often come from fear. Fear is very draining! **Fear is truly the major thing that holds us back in life.** Fear can cripple us. It stops us from taking action. Our fear stems from a lack of clarity about our personal value and power. Without fear, we are peaceful. We are not immediately on the defense. We are in a state of trust and **trust and fear cannot occupy the same space.**

Two opposing forces cannot occupy the same space. We cannot be experiencing fear (the absence of love) and trust (love) at the same time. I wrote this in a letter to my grandmother, "When you trust that's what you do; trust, just trust. You don't question the reason or the validity – you just trust."

When we feel confident in our ability to meet life's challenges with power and clarity we have no fear. Clarity leads us to being fearless, self-confident and powerful.

Whether there are only two intrinsic fears (falling and loud noises), the fact that we learn most fears is powerful information. **This means that if we learned fear we can also unlearn it!**

How? Being aware of the truth that we can unlearn fear, we can refuse to accept it any longer. Recognizing a negative behavior is one of the first steps to getting rid of it. Next time fear rears its ugly head consider if it is somehow "learned," knowing that in learning anything there is room for reconsideration. With some intelligent thought and use of a Positive Expectation Statement™, you may be able to rid yourself of this fear.

Life is full of illusion. I heard about a woman who is very afraid of bugs and another who has an overwhelming fear of thunder. Sometimes fear sounds like the voice of our own good intuition, when in truth it is a concept we have falsely learned that still plays in our head. We then reinforce it by further repetition.

The better we become at dealing with stress, eradicating worry, and disarming false fears, the less we confuse information we're hearing and the better we become at trusting ourselves.

Control and Trust

So often, we feel we need to control things. For some, insisting on control seems synonymous with taking responsibility. Yet, when we trust our higher power, we no longer feel this need. When we trust we feel things are already in control.

Dr. Denis Waitley explained in his book, *SEEDS OF GREATNESS*, about a University of California at Berkeley study indicating that the happiest, best-adjusted individuals are **those who believe** they have a strong measure of control over their lives, "They seem to choose appropriate responses to what occurs and to stand up to inevitable changes with less apprehension. They learn from their past mistakes, rather than replay them. They spend time 'doing' in the present, rather than fearing what may happen." *[Emphasis added.]*

They are in a state of trust. They allow themselves to relax into the force of nature where all is in a perfect state and, in control.

If you have been deeply hurt, you may find it difficult to trust again. Distrust often creates withdrawal, when we would be better jumping back into the pool of life to maintain our "trusting skills." Using our ability to trust wisely is a form of "positive thinking." It is belief our prayers will be answered. "Positive thinking" is not about forcing our will onto the universe to make something happen. It is about believing in the positive possibilities of life. It is about believing that what we ask for (or better) will happen.

It's just not always obvious, as our wanting what we want the way we want it clouds our vision. With trust in our petitions for a higher guidance the answer will come, and for our highest good. It may not look exactly how we thought it would look, or come about in the manner we expected, yet, the details are in the very process of your being by way of your thinking.

True Life Example: I believe I have great intuition about people, and yet, trusting other people has hurt me, too. Years ago, I trusted a man who became my fiancé – not once, but twice. Do I stutter? No, I do not. ☺ He betrayed me both times! Took my money, broke my heart, made me feel demeaned and foolish both times – you can imagine my hurt and anger. My only consolation was that I did not marry him – either time. After the second time however, my level of trust crashed.

If I was tuning in and listening, as I do, how did this happen? Finally, a wise counselor explained that there was nothing there for me to read. You see he was one of those amoral people; he had no morals for me to read. He was one who would have fooled anyone (even himself I came to realize) and he did – he even fooled my friends.

This was unusual so I know that I can still trust myself. Yes, even when we trust ourselves we can get hurt. It is unfair to judge other people by our past disappointments.

I believe that, as T. Harv Eker says, "It's all good." My understanding of this comment is that things always work for the best. How could my fiancé stealing from me be for the best? It kept me from marrying him! So, you see, it is "all good!"☺ He's long gone and my trust grows stronger and continues to serve me well. Clearly, disappointment may lead us to say a well deserved, "Good-bye," and in this case, in the words of that old country western song, "Thank God and Greyhound, He's Gone!"

GO WITH THE FLOW

Have the courage to trust in your higher power. Start by listening for that inner voice only you can hear. Personally, I think the voice I hear is that of my "rich and loving Father" who always comes through for me. I could tell you story after story of what some would call "miracles" in my life. I know now that so many things that seemed unfair at the time were experiences that enhanced my life.

How to Trust

1. **Be truthful**. Trust is best from truth. It is easy to trust when we are confident in the truth. So ask yourself if the issue at hand is based on truth, and is your response coming from your best self?
2. **Decide if you feel resistance** to the idea of this being truth. Perhaps it's something that would best be changed, at least somewhat. If so, change what you can.
3. **Disarm your own false fears**. Total control is illusionary so let go of resentments, move away from your ego and allow forgiveness.
4. **Relax into the trust**. Having discerned the truth and made your decision, you can now relax into trust, knowing that even without all of the details; you are moving toward your highest good.

I encourage you to open your heart to trusting so you discover it can be "all good." You will recognize the significance of the Happiness Action Tool™ of Trust in building your happiest life.

Positive Expectation Statement™

For Happiness Action Tool™ #12
THE SIGNIFICANCE OF TRUST

"I trust the process of life."

(6 words)

For free gifts to support you in being your happiest, visit your happiness community at TheHappinessCommunity.com.

CHAPTER FIFTEEN

To Thine Own Self Be True

HAPPINESS ACTION TOOL™ #13
THE STRENGTH OF INTEGRITY

"You are the master of your fate,
you are the captain of your soul."
~ William Ernest Henley

"Nothing is at last sacred but the integrity of your own mind."
~ Ralph Waldo Emerson

"Character is much easier kept than recovered."
~ Thomas Paine

Integrity is an amazing attribute. It impacts and adds strength to every area of our lives. William Shakespeare expressed, "This above all: to thine own self be true. And it must follow as the night the day, thou canst not then be false to any man."

When we live from integrity, we acknowledge that we are the force behind our life. Integrity allows us to develop self-esteem and happiness. Without it, we often sabotage ourselves.

Dan Millman said, "When we know deep down that we're acting with integrity despite impulses to do otherwise, we feel gates of higher energy and inspiration open inside of us." Ralph Waldo Emerson shared, "Every violation of truth is not only a sort of suicide in the liar, but is a stab at the health of human society."

My friend, Bill Matthews, appropriately said, "There is no such thing as part-time integrity!" To me integrity simply means always living up to my own highest standards; doing what is right for me as long as it does not harm anyone else.

Physician Emmett Miller said, "Integrity is the state of being complete and whole. When we have integrity, our thoughts, words, and actions are consistent with each other and reflect our professed philosophy and our deepest values."

Senator Alan Simpson said, "If you have integrity, nothing else matters. If you don't have integrity, nothing else matters."

With integrity, we act responsibly. The word responsible simply means "the ability to respond." What a wonderful ability.

Dr. Robert Anthony said, "The interesting thing is that you do not have to be superhuman or extraordinary to break loose from your limitations. There really is no such thing as a 'great' person. There are only 'ordinary' people who have decided to do 'great' things. Their desire to express their unlimited potential motivates them. Each day, they meet their problems head-on, overcoming them one at a time until they achieve their deepest desires. Instead of blaming others for their condition, they do something constructive about their situation. Apply this to yourself. Your personal freedom and innermost desires are waiting for you, but first, you must STAKE YOUR CLAIM!"

True Life Example: A few years ago, while having sushi at a restaurant in Rohnert Park, California, I met a remarkable couple, Bob and Barbara Brooks. Somehow, the conversation led Bob to tell us about how he became the owner of O.T.'s Barbeque Sauce.

Listening to his story, I realized it was his integrity had led him to this good fortune. It seems that while renovating a home they had purchased from a widow, they kept finding envelopes containing money. They saved them all until the remodeling was finished. By this time, there was a sum of $33,000! Now, this was a shocking thing, however not as shocking as what happened next in this amazing story. They gave every penny of that $33,000 back to the previous owner, the widow!

How did this make Bob Brooks the CEO and owner of the barbeque company? Seems that the family that owned the barbeque sauce recipe was looking for someone they felt they could trust to take the recipe and market it. When they read about the story of Bob Brooks and how he gave the money back, they knew they had found their "man." They knew they had found true integrity.

How is your integrity? To find, out just check your motivations and your intentions. **Living with integrity means that we do not compromise our values.** Doing something that would appear to be good but for the wrong reasons is not doing something with integrity. Doing something to impress or to please someone else (say a new love interest) that we would not otherwise do, is not living with integrity.

For example, if the new love in our life admires punctuality, and we manage to be on time when seeing him or her, even though we are habitually late for others, our motivations are wrong and we are not living with integrity. We are only being prompt to impress the other person, not really out of consideration for him or her. If we want to be on time more often, we can work on that – for ourselves.

I think it is worth looking at integrity versus morality. Morality, although based on ethics, is a judgment about something. It usually involves other people and includes our thoughts on their perception of our actions.

Living with integrity is living from personal ethics, whether other people live ethically or not, or are expecting us to. Oprah Winfrey said, **"Real integrity is doing the right thing, knowing that nobody's going to know whether you did it or not."** H. Jackson Brown, Jr. expressed the same thought, "Our character is what we do when we think no one is looking."

Don't make an effort to please others just for the sake of them liking you. Instead, please yourself – your **BEST** self by upholding and reinforcing your own values. As Anotole France put it, "The first virtue of all really great men is that they are sincere. They eradicate hypocrisy from their hearts."

It Feels Good to Be Responsible

Taking responsibility is difficult for some people. When we accept responsibility for our attitude, we have to admit it's a

decision for us **to continue** our bad behavior, as well as our negative attitudes.

However, when we can, we free ourselves to accept feeling good as a choice, too. So, if we really want to feel good, we can. We can accept feeling good as a choice and know we are responsible for the richness of our core prosperity. Winston Churchill believed that, "The price of greatness is responsibility."

Dorothy Corkille Briggs in *CELEBRATE YOUR SELF*, said, "If we own up to the fact that we choose, we force ourselves to look squarely at why we continue self-defeating choices."

Dr. Robert Anthony put it this way, "If you are constantly being mistreated, you're cooperating with the treatment." He also said, "Maturity consists of no longer being taken in by one's self." He explained, "Once you realize you have given your power away, you can make the decision to take it back."

Make an Agreement with Yourself

Living from integrity and acting responsibly gives that satisfactory feeling of being in control. By making an agreement with our self to act responsibly, we lay an important foundation for accomplishing almost anything in life. This means we are making a commitment to live our lives the best way possible and, let's face it, living the best way possible feels very good.

Why do we avoid responsibility? Possibly, because we are afraid that we won't be able to live up to the expectations we *perceive* are attached to it, we associate responsibility with what we think other people expect of us.

It's bad enough we sometimes have such high expectations of ourselves however, couple that with our perceived expectations from others, and we become really stressed. "Expectations" are often the fuel for stress. Making your choices from integrity will dramatically ease that stress.

Mark Twain encouraged us to, "Always do right; this will gratify some and astonish the rest." He also said, "It is curious that physical courage should be so common in the world and moral courage so rare." Brian Tracy said it well, "The happiest people in the world are those who feel absolutely terrific about themselves, and this is the natural outgrowth of accepting total responsibility for every part of their life."

By now, I'm sure we'd agree that most fear is a perception. Remember the well-known acronym for fear: FALSE EVIDENCE APPEARING REAL.

So, move past the fear aspect and focus more on the positives of responsibility. Commitment goes hand in hand with integrity and responsibility. You make a commitment to *yourself* when you decide to be responsible about something, and when you act responsibly you are keeping your commitments to yourself and others. You'll get a double dose of happiness for keeping your promises **and** behaving responsibly.

Commitments Are With Yourself

You can promise anyone anything. Yet, if in your heart you do not mean that promise, you probably will not keep it. Look at your intent. Ultimately, **we always make any commitment with ourselves**.

It bears repeating what Shakespeare said in *HAMLET,* "This above all, to thine own self be true, and it must follow, as the night the day, thou canst not then be false to any man." The opposite is also true; if we are not true to ourselves, it will be difficult to be reliable to others. Moreover, if we are not true to others, how can we count on ourselves, for ourselves?

A commitment is simply a promise – a promise we make to ourselves – and, promises aren't meant to be broken. ☺ People with true integrity finish what they begin from a heart-felt decision. They will do everything within their power not to desert a project mid-stream. Do you keep your promises?

We've all heard the motto, "If it's to be, it's up to me." This means we don't see ourselves as victims. We know it's not someone or something outside of us preventing us from succeeding. We are giving away our personal power. Take it back now!

Dr. Robert Anthony emphasized, "As long as we feel victimized we give up our power to change." He explained, "The only thing you have no choice about is making choices."

Les Brown knows firsthand that it's true that he has more control over his life than anyone else does. He was labeled "educable mentally retarded" after his parents give him up at birth. Fortunately, a high school teacher told him that, **"someone else's opinion of you does not have to become your reality."** He went on to become an Ohio state legislator, an author and a top motivational speaker.

In his words, "If you take responsibility for yourself you will develop a hunger to accomplish your dreams." He also said, "Honor your commitments with integrity."

Respond Don't React

The most important effect on the outcome of our lives is how we **respond** to what happens to us – *not* how we **react** to it. **We have greater control by responding, rather than reacting to what is going on.** "Respons" is how the word responsible begins. When we are responsible, we respond, instead of react.

Jack Canfield and Georgia Noble explained in *LEARNING TO LOVE & EMPOWER YOURSELF*, that earlier events plus our responses equal the outcome of self-esteem (earlier events + responses = self-esteem). Take a step back and respond, not react, to gain great self-esteem from positive outcomes.

Consider the difference between the two words "react" and "respond." A reaction is automatic; we just do it without considering the outcome. A response, however, has prior thought attached to it.

Respond knowing you have considered your options before making the decision to take the action you do. Staying in integrity will enhance our self-worth as well as allow us to respond rather than to react to situations regardless of what is going on around us.

Knowing we are in control of most of the circumstances in our lives, we don't react emotionally to everything we interpret as a threat. Instead, we blend left-brain logic with right-brain intuition resulting in constructive responses.

Put Yourself First

Prioritizing your obligations assists you in being your most effective. This can be simple if you always keep the important concept in mind that you are your most important priority. You always need to put yourself first. **You can only be good for someone else if you are good for yourself. We can only give if we have something to give.**

So, love yourself and take good care of yourself. If you are fulfilled you will automatically have love overflowing. Once we care for ourselves, caring for others becomes effortless and natural. When we feel nurtured and happy we want to share. We share authentically, not because we feel we "should."

Knowing we can rely on ourselves, we feel worthwhile and have that great feeling of self-reliance and we become a trillionaire in core prosperity. We are empowered.

True Life Example: I remember a time that empowered me and enhanced my sense of accomplishment. I was in college and since my mother had moved out of the area, I had simply assumed my Grandmother would be delighted to have me stay with her over the summer. I was panic stricken when I learned this was not the case.

I also remember, the sense of personal power I felt when I found a place to live *and* a job to pay for the place. Ever since I have known I can take care of myself! I gained a tremendous sense of self-reliance, and as I a truth that sometimes what we see as a creative challenge is a blessing in disguise!

Have Realistic Expectations of Yourself

To be responsible be realistic about your current capabilities and honest with yourself about how you intend to use those capabilities and your time. Making a commitment you know in advance that you cannot keep insures disappointment for everyone involved.

Life does come at us quickly sometimes and "things do happen" that can change our plans leaving even the most prepared of us helpless to follow through. Just don't start out by making promises that surpass realistic expectations. If you expect too much of yourself you set yourself up to fail.

Realistic expectations allow us to win. **All we can ever do is the best we can.** Making it okay to decide to simply do the best we can, we will do just that. We will do the best we can! What's great is that the best we can do is often much more than we anticipated, and what an added surprise that can be.

We Can Control Our Reaction

People with weak self-esteem seem to believe that life just happens to them. They feel like pawns of fate. To these people life is a series of unpredictable events.

People with high self-esteem, however, embrace the idea that we are all primarily responsible for causing our own effect in life. We all know we cannot control everything in life – it's for sure we cannot control other people.

If there is anything we can control, it is how we choose to be. We can usually control our time. We can control whom we have in our life. We can control what we say. We can control what we decide to do. We can decide what goals we set in life. We can even control our emotions. In fact, when all is "said and done," for anything that appears to "just happen to us" – anything that we think we cannot control – we can always control how we respond to it!

People Energize or Drain Us

We, therefore, are responsible for the majority of results in our lives. Take for instance, the people you choose to have in your life. As we discussed before, people either energize or drain us. For the sake of simplicity, if someone has no effect on us we will just leave those people out of this example.

Look at each person in your life and see if he or she adds to – or takes away from it. Realize that even the people who energize you most of the time do occasionally drain you. Yet, some people in your life are psychic vampires. Why are they even in your life?

It's a matter of percentages – do they add to or take away from your life more often. If they are taking away from your life – is it that they feed off you, or do they just draw you out (which actually can be uncomfortable yet growth enhancing)?

You may also have people in your life with likeable characteristics that drain you regularly, hold you down, or even depress you with their negativity. Perhaps it's time to re-assess their being a part of your close, intimate circle of friends.

If people drain us more often than they energize us perhaps it is time to release them, leaving more time for the people we truly love and who energize us!

True Life Example: After realizing that people either drain us or energize us, I decided to look at every significant person in my life and determine if he or she energized or drained me more. I knew it would be best if I let go of the people who drained me. The trick is to determine which side of the scale they fall on. My boyfriend was waiting for me at home. One guess as to who was the first to go. ☺ Who's draining you? Who's energizing you?

The Responsibility of Being Here Now

Action is NOW. When we are taking action we are in the present – we are doing it NOW.

Being in the present, we live our lives with full impact. Our self-esteem is high as we feel in control and this leads to us feeling peaceful.

So, take responsibility for being present, each-and-every minute of each-and-every hour of each-and-every day! This is the ultimate display of authenticity and integrity – that of living in the now fully present and accountable.

Enhanced Productivity from Feeling Attractive

Case Study: Barbara L. Fredrickson, a social psychologist, reported that in a study of 350 men and women, "there is significant evidence that proves that when one feels unattractive, it produces diminished mental performance especially when it comes to performing demanding tasks such as solving advanced math problems. A poor self-image brings about low productivity."

She continued, "I'm sure you know this to be true in your own experience. Recall a day when you felt you were looking particularly great – do you remember how people responded favorably to you, how empowered you felt, how productive you became as a result? Now, recall a day when you felt you weren't looking particularly attractive. Do you remember how indifferently people responded to you, how underpowered you felt, how you moped and became unproductive in the process? Enough said. The pursuit of physical attractiveness has now been elevated to a necessity."

Dr. Denis Waitley said, "No matter how confident or sure of ourselves we try to appear, we still project on the outside how we feel about ourselves on the inside. For example, when we aren't feeling well physically, we don't look well at the skin or surface level.

He further shared these words, "Correspondingly, when we don't feel good about ourselves emotionally or mentally, we don't seem to make a very good impression with our looks, personal grooming and conversation. A first step in good communications is a good appearance. It is the way to gain the attention of people who are important to us long enough to project our inside value, like a good book among the thousands available on the bookstore shelf."

So, take responsibility for your image, knowing when you look good you have an advantage. The way we look and express ourselves is our calling card. It's how people remember us. The visual is what we first share with others. What do you want to share with others?

Being confident you present a good image, you aren't preoccupied with the anxiety of how others perceive you, and you actually project an even more appealing image. By being comfortably who you are, you enjoy the point of the occasion.

Allowing yourself to focus some of your time and energy into this area of your life, you end up freeing your time for more productive activities. People do make decisions about us based on our image. If we are dressed appropriately for the situation, people will tend to trust our decisions. Clean and dressed neatly, people will assume that we respect ourselves, and, that, in turn, we respect them.

"Beauty is in the Eye of the Beholder"

It's more than how we look on the outside, and it's certainly not about looking perfect or wearing thousand dollar suits.☺ **Inside beauty *IS* ultimately more important than outer beauty.**

As well, beauty really *IS* in the eye of the beholder. It is a personal opinion.

In fact, enthusiasm attracts as much as beauty *ever* could! When we radiate enthusiasm, the kind that is both joyful and intelligent, the energy of it lights up our face, our smile, and the entire room, and this, in turn, attracts all wonders of marvelous things to us!

Did you know that people who stand up straight are perceived as more intelligent as well as attractive? According to Andrew J. Dubrin, author of *PERSONAL MAGNETISM*, "They radiate confidence and magnetism, and these are all qualities that draw people to them."

Stand up tall and show others you like yourself. Give them reason to believe they will like you, too.

Magnifying the things you like about your looks will minimize those you don't like. If you feel your eyes are one of your best features, and that your lips are too small, then draw attention to your eyes.

TO THINE OWN SELF BE TRUE

We all have things about ourselves that we like and dislike. Choose to concentrate on your positive features. And, for heaven sakes, don't point out your faults – **most people are not as critical of us as we are of ourselves**.

If there *is* something you don't like about yourself that you can change, then do it. If it's something you can't change, find something that you do like about yourself and build on that. This will refocus you from dwelling on what you don't like.

For example, if you don't like your hair then get a new cut or change the color. There's also the chance that you are being your own worst critic. You may have an appeal you are not aware of yet.

True Life Example: I had pictures taken at Glamour Shots Photo Studios for this book and our website. It was really a lot of fun to go and feel like I was some kind of model as they directed me into many different poses for numerous shots. They specialize in making you look your best, so my pictures turned out well. I plan to frame one so that I can visualize myself at my very best. Perhaps you want to go to Glamour Shots so you can feel like a star, too, and have a visual reminder of your best looking self.

Please understand that I really believe that **we are all worthy human beings no matter what we look like!** Outward things do not reflect our true core self and inner beauty. They are just outward appearances.

Looking and feeling our best we forget ourselves; allowing us to concentrate on things that are more important than how we look. Present the best "you" possible and lovingly accept the rest. It's who we are, not what we look like, that truly matters, and outshines all the exterior trappings.

It is true though that the visual is what we first share. So, what is it you want to share with others about you?

Cecil B. De Mille said, "Remember you are a star. Never go across the alley even to dump garbage unless you are dressed to the teeth." Remember to brush your teeth, too. ☺

Still, it's worth noting, as Brian Tracy said that, "Confidence on the outside comes from integrity on the inside" Being dressed to the teeth will never cover up negative attitude.

Good Health is Imperative

Important to living with integrity is taking care of our health. An Arabian Proverb says, "He who has health has hope; and he who has hope, has everything."

I especially like this Spanish Proverb, **"A man too busy to take care of his health is like a mechanic too busy to take care of his tools."**

If we don't feel good, how can we expect to function optimally? Pain can be very distracting. In fact, it can be absolutely crippling. It's been proven that toxins in our body even affect our brain function and resulting in us not living to our fullest.

It amazes me that **some people spend a lot of time and money to improve their outer appearance yet, they give little attention to their health and nutrition.** One of the most important things you can do to look good is to drink plenty of water, get enough sleep and have proper nutrition.

We are careful what type of gasoline we put in our cars. Do we care as much for ourselves? We grab fast food and eat it quickly, usually with no regard for the nutritional value to our bodies. We also seem to think we can get by without proper sleep.

Our body will eventually let us know it doesn't like to be mistreated. **Just like our automobile, our body needs proper fuel and maintenance or it will break down!**

Please, please, please, understand how important your health is. Emerson said, "**The first wealth is health**." It won't mean anything if you are famous and have a lot of money if you are in pain or suffering ill health.

You may not be as interested in nutrition as I am. However, just paying attention to the basics, like drinking more water and eating more fruits and vegetables (and not as a side dish to your junk food☺), will greatly enhance your health. How can you expect to be happy if you are sick and/or tired?

> As a side note: Many of our foods are genetically altered, so we are not getting the same benefits we used to. Our foods are also wrought with pesticides, additives and many nasty chemicals that our body has to fight against to stay healthy.

Start paying attention to what is in your food. It is your fuel. You deserve to feed yourself premium grade food!

Your may also want to add premium grade water to your diet. I have been drinking alkaline water to balance the pH of my body for several years now – and I truly believe this has given me a much higher quality of life. It cured the pain of arthritis and stopped the gas and bloating I was experiencing. Most importantly, it also helped relieve my feelings of anxiety, which had caused me to cry at the drop of a hat.

So listen to "Dr. Gayleen" ☺ and eat good food, drink alkaline balanced water and exercise. Your body will thank you for it, you will feel and look better, and you will be happier!

True Life Example: You may have heard of a "runner's high." Scientists tell us this is because exercise raises the level of endorphins (happy hormones) in the brain.

My friend, Dave Murphy, told me that if he feels concerned about something just getting his heart rate up by exercising helps him feel different about things. "Things aren't any different, but I find my feelings about them are different."

His responses are, therefore, different. ☺ Ah, the power of those little endorphins that give us a "happy high."

Integrity Means No Excuses

People can be so creative with their excuses. Too bad we don't use that creativity to find a way to do whatever it is we are probably avoiding in the first place. You see, true integrity is with one's self and we can choose to live our lives without making excuses.

> Side note: It is my belief that if criminals used their same creative energy with integrity, not only would they actually profit more (both monetarily and emotionally), they would eliminate their need to choose a life of crime in the first place.

The concept of integrity and responsibility, especially for our choices, is very much about cause and effect. The Reverend James Smith, a good friend of my friend and writing partner, Linda Hancock Moore, told her a great story that applies here. He said, "I told my children and now I tell my grandchildren, 'There are two kinds of choices you can make; you can choose right and you can choose wrong, but if you choose wrong, you'll always be looking over your shoulder.'"

The thing that really matters is the kind of person we are. It is about how we live our lives. It is about living a life of integrity by taking responsibility for every decision we make.

From a life of integrity, you will fill your life with uplifting information and live in balance, helping when you can, surrounding yourself with people and things that bring you peace, love and happiness. As the old adage says, "You get what you give."

As Ken Blanchard put it, "Honesty is telling the truth to ourselves and others. Integrity is living that truth." Sanaya Roman and Duane Packer encouraged us, "Honor your integrity and you will be repaid many times over with increased prosperity."

As Carl von Ossietzky expressed, "We cannot appeal to the conscience of the world when our own conscience is asleep." R. Buckminster Fuller shared, "If humanity does not opt for integrity we are through completely."

Grover Cleveland expressed it well, "Unswerving loyalty to duty, constant devotion to truth, and a clear conscience will overcome every discouragement and surely lead the way to usefulness and high achievement."

The quote by Ralph Waldo Emerson at the beginning of this chapter is worth repeating, "Nothing is at last sacred but the integrity of your own mind."

How to Stay in Integrity

1. **Check your intentions.** Are you doing this only for show? Would you do the same if the eyes of all you cared for were on you? Does what you are doing honor the best in life as well as the best of you? Are you listening to old tapes in your head, or a higher set of values? Does it take in the highest good of all involved? Does it foster positive emotions: love, courage, gratitude, generosity and forgiveness?
2. **Check in with your higher self.** If you feel uncomfortable about your decision, you are probably not working with integrity.
3. **To thine own self be true.** If you are not being honest with yourself, it is all a con, and there can be no integrity there. Living as a human sacrifice is not living out of integrity.
4. **Only act with everyone's best interest in mind.**
5. **Live without guilt or regrets.** Work honestly and play lovingly to build an exemplary life with integrity.

Live with integrity and you will attract the best to you. Then you can smile, knowing you have the strength of integrity to build your happiest life.

Positive Expectation Statement™

For Happiness Action Tool™ #13
THE STRENGTH OF INTEGRITY

"My actions reflect my best self."

(6 words)

For free gifts to support you in being your happiest, visit your happiness community at TheHappinessCommunity.com.

CHAPTER SIXTEEN

Eliminate the Brushfires

HAPPINESS ACTION TOOL™ #14
THE BENEFIT OF ORGANIZATION

"Dost thou love life? Then do not squander time, for that's the stuff life is made of."
~ Benjamin Franklin

"Routine is not organization, any more than paralysis is order."
~ Arthur Helps

"It's a matter of reducing the work to its very simplest possible state, eliminating all of the things that lead away from the guts of the work, the thing the work is really about. Anything that's there must build towards its over-all organization and meaning."
~ Paul Cullen

"A messy environment reflects a confused mind."
~ Gayleen Williams

Some people find it odd that I love to throw, or give things away. It gives me a wonderful sense of accomplishment.

It's a universal truth that creating a vacuum in our life works like a magnet to bring new and interesting things in to fill the void. This works with people as well as with things. Why waste time, since it is so precious, on the unwanted or unnecessary?

This also relates to the people in your life, as well the things. Do the people in your life drain you or energize you. Why waste time on the unnecessary, or even worse, the negative?

Get rid of the people who drain you so you have time to enjoy the people who add to your life! (And, yes, I do know I said this already! It's just worth repeating. ☺)

Time Management is Life Management

Time is very precious and to be valued. M. Scott Peck shared, "Until you value yourself, you will not value your time. Until you value your time, you will not do anything with it." Alan Lakein said, "Time is life. It is irreversible and irreplaceable. To waste your time is to waste your life, but to master your time is to master your life and make the most of it."

Helen Weidner said, "Get rid of the stuff. Live lean, so as to have time to enjoy people instead of things." Make full use of your time so you live life as completely as possible. It's said that time management is life management. By managing your time, you will have more time for the positive things in your life.

An unknown author told us, "One thing you can't recycle is wasted time." Harvey MacKay shared, "You can save time, spend time, kill time, need time, hide time, lose time, even try to buy time. But the simple fact is that once time is past, you can't get it back."

The best advice for time management is to focus on results, not just on being busy! Concentrate on meeting deadlines and finding what you need easily.

Is your life so overwhelming that you never feel any satisfaction? If so, it's time to start weeding out some things. I guarantee not everything in your life is so important you have to keep it. Elaine St. James shared, "**Maintaining a complicated life is a great way to avoid changing it**." Many times people focus on meaningless tasks as a way of avoiding life. It's about simplifying your life so you can focus on and enjoy the people and things that are most valuable to you. Being organized enhances the quality of your life.

Disorganized people stay busy, having to put out brushfires. Crisis after crisis seem to come into their life. Eliminate the clutter and you will eliminate the unnecessary brushfires in life. Priscilla Elfrey said, **"If we do not eliminate the clutter, the clutter will eliminate us."** A great way to get rid of things is to ask, "If there were a fire and I lost this or this, which would be more important?"

How to Get Organized

Simplify Your Life

1. **Clean your clothes closet**. Do you really wear all of those clothes? Get rid of what you haven't worn in the last year.
2. **Clean your food pantry**. Help feed the hungry by giving away what you won't eat. You will find what is in the cupboard more easily.
3. **Clear your desk**. A cluttered desk causes one to become distracted; an organized one helps us focus on the task-at-hand.
4. **Set up a simple file system**. An accountant taught me a quick and easy method for easily filing paid bills and receipts; simply put them all together in a file for each month.
5. **Color-code your files**. I use colored plastic files or envelopes to group information about different subjects or projects.
6. **Purge your files**. At least once a year purge your files. Scan information into your computer. Use the "favorites" or "bookmarks" link in your computer's browser. You'll feel so much lighter.☺
7. **Write it down**. Don't rely on your memory. (Uh, where was I? Oh yeah, that 's right.) Keep an appointment calendar and a "to-do" list. I have combined these into one daily sheet showing who I need to contact, what I need to do and where I need to go. It also has a space for notes so that I can remember important extras, like birthdays. I include a pretty picture so it's visually more appealing and fun to use.
8. **Use a greeting card organizer with** 12 monthly folders, whether it's in the form of a box or a notebook. You will be prepared for upcoming events and be able to find them easily. It's also a great excuse for hanging out in the greeting card isle.☺
9. **Store similar items together** in clear plastic boxes for protection and easy retrieval. I use them to store holiday supplies, i.e., Valentine's Day, Easter, Christmas, and summer outdoor supplies. I also use them to store medical supplies. I have a sewing box, a hair care box and a memory box just to name a few. You get the idea.
10. **Put things away every day**. Either take a minute to put it away then or schedule 10 minutes each day to put things away. This will keep your life less cluttered and let you find things readily.
11. **Toss out old reading material**. Toss out outdated newspapers and catalogs more than three months old. Tear out articles you want to read or keep and toss the rest. You will find that you will get to read more of what is remaining because it will seem less overwhelming.

The goal is to simplify your life so you can focus on the most beneficial things in life. I believe that some people surround themselves with stuff trying to fill the emptiness they feel inside themselves. No amount of material things will ever take care of that sense of lack. **I believe that a messy environment reflects a confused mind.**

It's More Than Being Neat and Tidy

We tend to think of organization as being neat and tidy; that is only one part of it. We can be organized with the things in our life, however what about the ideas and project we need and/or want to put into action? How are your time management skills?

I am very good at organizing things and less organized with ideas and projects. I could use a coach in this area of my life. For you it might be the other way around. There is nothing wrong with asking for help.

Florynce Kennedy said it well, "Don't agonize. Organize." Stephanie Winston put it this way, "Getting organized is not an end in itself; it is a means to get where you want to be."

If you commit to at least one of the organization action tools shown above every day you will quickly see results and therefore, see how easy it is to be organized, and live your happiest life.

Positive Expectation Statement™

For Happiness Action Tool™ #14
THE BENEFIT OF ORGANIZATION

"I enjoy the benefits of being organized."

(7 words)

For free gifts to support you in being your happiest, visit your happiness community at TheHappinessCommunity.com

CHAPTER SEVENTEEN

Think: What Box?

HAPPINESS ACTION TOOL™ #15
THE GENIUS OF CREATIVITY

"One can resist the invasion of an army;
one cannot resist the invasion of ideas."
~ Victor Hugo

"The secret of not having worries, for me at least, is to have ideas."
~ Eugene Delacroix

"What is now proved was once only imagined."
~ William Blake

Creativity brings happiness. Just being creative puts us in a state of happiness. As Franklin D. Roosevelt put it, "Happiness lies in the joy of achievement and the thrill of creative effort."

Mary Lou Cook shared that, "Creativity is inventing, experimenting, growing, taking risks, breaking rules, making mistakes, and having fun." Yes, being creative is fun. Yet, it can also be serious business, very serious business. Creativity drives us to success. People who do not allow their creativity to express itself feel stifled and unhappy.

Without creativity, there would be no books, music, art, architecture or inventions. So many things would not have happened if there were no creativity. Creativity is imagination in action. Almost anything is possible when we employ creativity and imagination.

Albert Einstein shared his view that, "Without creative personalities able to think and judge independently, the upward development of society is unthinkable."

Arthur Combs, Ph.D. pointed out that, "Our whole educational system is built on 'right answers,' which produces a fear of making mistakes and stifles creativity." It's a shame that we limit our future by limiting the imaginations of our youth by taking art and music out of regular school curricula. Of course, education itself does bring an expanded canvas and more colorful pallet with which to facilitate our creativity. It's a good idea to keep our imagination handy either way. ☺

Dave Lakani, creator of Rapid Ideation Processing Marketing Geonomics, shared, "Ideas are the product of connections, both logical and illogical. Effective creativity is a merger of these logical and illogical thoughts together to form revolutionary new strategies and plans. Sadly, most Americans focus only on what has already been developed by others."

An unknown author shared, very powerfully, "Imagination enlarges the vision, stretches the mind, challenges the impossible. You awaken your imagination through the driving power of curiosity and discontent. Your imagination becomes for you a magic lamp with which to explore the darkness of the unknown that you may chart new paths to old goals. Through imagination, you touch and express the power of the infinite. You reach into the heaven to grasp an idea, then you bring it down to earth and make it work."

Creativity is a Universal Trait

Contrary to what many believe, **we are all creative.** Creativity is not something that only a few extraordinary individuals possess. We just may express it differently. Creativity is not limited to what we think of as the traditional "creative fields" such as the arts. Is the writer less talented than the artist who sculpts? Is the sculptor less talented than the mechanic or engineer who can build a car? Is the mechanic less talented than the singer, dancer or actor? Who's to say? I say, thank God for such a wonderful diversity of talent.

True Life Example: I grew up in Laguna Beach, known world over for being an artist's colony. All of this boundless beauty intimidated me. I couldn't draw a straight line so I thought that I wasn't an artist. Fortunately, in high school I had an art teacher who said, "Art is the expression of a person's feelings. You feel, therefore you are an artist." He freed my creativity with that statement and I thank him to this day. I have not become a great painter or sculptor; however, the thought applies to any form of artistic endeavor or form of creativity. I might not have written this book without this freedom of expression.

Albert Einstein expressed, **"Creativity is simply making something new or rearranging the old in a new way."** We don't have to be Einstein or Edison to come up with fresh ideas. Unlock your imagination and unleash your creativity. Allow yourself to be open to new and/or different ideas. Call upon the experience and expertise of other people, listen to their ideas and brainstorm with them. Allow yourself quiet time to hear your own creative ideas.

Natalie Goldberg expressed, "If you're having difficulty coming up with new ideas, then slow down. For me, slowing down has been a tremendous source of creativity. It has allowed me to open up – to know that there's life under the earth and that I have to let it come through me in a new way. Creativity exists in the present moment. You can't find it anywhere else."

"Think outside the box," is an expression associated with creativity. What if there wasn't a box? A box limits the imagination. Instead, think of a vast universe where anything is possible! That opens up all the possibilities! The first time Dell Morgan heard someone say to "think outside the box" she thought, "What box?"

True Life Example: One of my favorite posters is from a collection put out by Simpson Paper Company featuring a group of commissioned graphic designers. There were many brilliant examples of creativity; however, James Cross designed my very favorite. Done on a black background, the top half of the poster is a colorful fingerprint, while the bottom half is a gray bar code with a few words at the top that explain his premise that artificial intelligence will never replace the human touch. Find the entire words from the poster at TheHappinessCommunity.com.

A Squashed Bug

When we are young, we are more naturally creative because we allow our minds to run free. Roger von Oech, who wrote the book entitled *A WHACK ON THE SIDE OF THE HEAD*, asked what we might see if he held up a sheet of white paper and put a black dot on it with his pen? He said he has used this demonstration on thousands of adults in the seminars he has run and invariably he got the same answer: "A black dot." Asked of a kindergarten class he said a forest of hands shot up. "A Mexican hat," piped one kid. "Naw, that's a burnt hamburger," said another. "A squashed bug," observed a third.

Creative thinking can enhance all of our life experiences. Creativity can assist us in solving problems more effectively and faster, stimulate our intellect and bring personal satisfaction.

Fortunately, creativity isn't mysterious. Nobel Prize-winning Physician Albert Szent Gyorgyi shared with us, "Discovery consists of seeing what everybody has seen and thinking what nobody has thought."

"How do we start 'thinking what nobody else has thought?" asked von Oech. "Usually it takes a whack on the head, like Newton supposedly had when an apple striking his skull awakened him to the laws of gravity. Whacks can range from something as major as losing a job to something as trivial as wanting an unusual entrée for a dinner party."

"The idea that creativity spontaneously bubbles up from a magical well or gains a direct line to the Muses is just another myth among many about highly creative people and their work," said psychologist David Perkins, Co-director of Project Zero, a Harvard educational research project. The website for the project explains that the mission is, "to understand and enhance learning, thinking and creativity in the arts, as well as humanistic and scientific disciplines, at the individual and institutional levels," He added, "Momentary flashes of insight, often accompanied by images, make up only a small part of the creative process."

"Scholastic skills do not predict whether a person can create something that will make a difference in society or even in his or her own life," Project Co-director Howard Gardner said. There are ample historic examples of creative individuals who had little interest in school, or who were poor students. Benjamin Franklin had difficulty with math. Thomas Edison was at the bottom of his class. William Butler Yeats and George Bernard Shaw were both poor spellers." It sounds like we don't need to be intelligent to be creative. Now there's a happy thought!

Case Study: Often creativity is associated with intelligence. However, *intuition* is more important to the creative process than rational thought. Frank Barron, a psychologist, observed and measured creativity for forty plus years. "You don't have to have a high IQ to be intuitive," he explained. "Intuition depends less on the reasoning and verbal comprehension (the main measure of IQ) than it does on feelings and metaphor."

A Creative High

Exercise and other physical activity releases endorphins, the brain's natural opiates, putting us into what neuroscientist Candace Pert at the National Institute of Mental Health, called an "endorphinergic state" or a kind of altered state. As she shared, "The fun of exercise is being blitzed for days afterward."

Some people experience a burst of creativity or a "creative high." Creativity, according to Pert, comes from "the spiritual realm, the collective consciousness. And the mind is in a different realm than the molecules of the brain. The brain is a receiver, not the source."

Harvard's David Perkins developed what he called the "snowflake model of creativity." Like the snowflake with six sides, Perkins' model consists of six related but distinct psychological traits of the creative person. Creative people may not possess all six, Perkins said; the more they have the more creative they tend to be. According to him, these traits are a drive toward simplicity, and the ability to excel in finding problems, mental mobility, a willingness to take risks, objectivity, and inner motivation.

How to Inspire Creativity

1. **Keep track of your ideas**. Creative ideas often come at strange times, such as when doing monotonous things like blow-drying your hair or driving long distances, and may never come again. Keep a notepad handy to capture your creative ideas.
2. **Be open to ideas**. Ask questions. Don't dismiss an idea too quickly. Give it time to gestate. The idea that at first may seem silly might be just the idea you need.
3. **Be aware**. Pay attention to things you wouldn't ordinarily. Look for ideas in things, experiences, people, and random thoughts that cross your mind. Look for how you might change them, even just slightly.
4. **Honor your hunches**. Don't put down your ideas as nonsense. Listen to your intuition. Be especially receptive when you are in a relaxed state. Many creative thoughts come upon awakening. Keep paper and pen by your bed to capture those creative ideas.
5. **Pursue hobbies**. Hobbies tune-up our creative skills and they also relax us. More importantly, they can inspire us by igniting our interests and passions, leading us to productive outcomes, perhaps even new and exciting careers.
6. **Be willing to take risks**. As Dr. Robert Anthony says, "the biggest risk is not taking a risk." Management consultant, Chester Barnard, said it incredibly well: "To try and fail, is a least to learn. To fail to try is to suffer the inestimable loss of what might have been."

Fortunately, as Maya Angelou pointed out, "You cannot use up creativity. The more you use, the more you have." Pursue your genius of creativity to live your happiest life.

Positive Expectation Statement™

For Happiness Action Tool™ #15
THE GENIUS OF CREATIVITY

"I enjoy allowing my creative genius."

(6 words)

For free gifts to support you in being your happiest, visit your happiness community at TheHappinessCommunity.com.

CHAPTER EIGHTEEN

Reshape the Future

HAPPINESS ACTION TOOL™ #16
The Wonder of Imagination

"First, it is ridiculed. Second, it is violently opposed. Third, it is accepted as being self-evident."
~ Arthur Schopenhauer

"The possibilities slow fuse is lit by the Imagination."
~ Emily Dickinson

"I like the dreams of the future better than the history of the past."
~ Thomas Jefferson

My mother used to tell me, **"If you can see yourself doing something you can do it."** I know now she was paraphrasing the famous saying by Napoleon Hill, "Whatever man can conceive mentally, he can bring into reality."

The act of believing is tremendously powerful, especially when fueled by vivid imagination and detailed visualization. If we truly believe we can do it, we can bring whatever we imagine to life. If we believe we can do it we can. The power is in the belief. The power of belief enables a person to do what others may claim is impossible.

My mother's comment would have only been stronger if she had also said to feel yourself doing it; feel yourself in the picture. It's best to foster a mental image by holding it in your mind's eye and feeling as if it is happening right then.

The secret is to keep adding details, making it more and more accurate, and therefore, more and more real. If we picture it and feel it as real long enough that computer we call our brains will accept the input as true!

Research has proven that the mind cannot tell the difference between something that has really happened and something imagined. **An event vividly experienced in our mind is recorded in our memory bank as an actual experience.**

I'm not sure who to credit with the "IxV=R Principle." (Imagination mixed with Vividness becomes Reality.) It's said that our mind thinks in pictures, not words. If we vividly picture in our mind what we desire it will become a reality.

Remember, to make this most effective we need to "feel" ourselves in the picture, which enhances our 'believing" as we utilize mental rehearsal. You see, we don't make mistakes in our mind. We really can picture our way to success – especially if we add as much feeling to the picture as possible.

Mark Victor Hansen shared these powerful words, "We have 18 billion brain cells, just waiting for us to give them direction. The only limitations that exist are those we impose on ourselves. Otherwise, our brains do not know limitations. Our minds will believe what we convince them to believe. So why aren't we living out our dreams?"

Research Verifies the Power of Imagination

Case Study: **Researchers discovered some years ago that using our imagination or "mental imaging" could be a powerful tool in the control of pain, depression, fear, disease and insomnia.** In an experiment reported in the *JOURNAL OF MENTAL IMAGERY*, conducted at the University of Lowell in Massachusetts, Cognitive Psychologist Robert Kunzendorf did a study that supports the belief that the brain does not know the difference between fact and fiction. He found that 5 of his 20 subjects were especially capable of producing explicit mental pictures. Kunzendorf had all 20 participants hooked to electrodes and instructed them to look at various flashing colored lights. He found that each color affected the retina in a different way, each producing a specific pattern.

Then Kunzendorf requested the 5 subjects who fantasized best to imagine the colors (rather than look at the actual colored lights). The imagined colors produced the same effects on the eye as the "real" colors. Interestingly, these color imagers also tended to be the most capable of altering their hand temperatures and heart rates.

Case Study: Jonathan Parker of MentalStrength.com, said, "A study conducted in 1991 found that there was no age barrier to imagination and visualization. The research involved 120 7th-grade field hockey players. The study organized the players into two groups. Group A combined relaxation plus imagery (visualization) with the normal physical practice, while Group B practiced as they normally do with just physical practice. The players in Group A, the relaxation/imagery group, improved their accuracy in hitting field-hockey targets by 160%! Those in Group B, participated only in physical practice, improved as well, but by less than half as much, for a 70% improvement."

Why is this so? Well as we discussed above the subconscious cannot tell the difference between a real experience and one just imagined vividly. Both the medical and scientific communities agree that **visualized images actually bring about psychological and physiological changes to virtually the same degree as direct experience.** Albert Einstein pointed out that, "Imagination is more important than knowledge."

Case Study: Dr. Herbert Benson, Associate Professor of Medicine at Harvard Medical School, who has earned international recognition for many years of research into the power of the mind over matter, witnessed an incredible feat.

He was able to see 12 Tibetan Buddhist monks gather in a chilly room at the beckoning of the Dalai Lama. Each monk wrapped himself in a cotton sheet that had been dipped into a bucket of ice-cold water. The monks closed their eyes and began to meditate. Within minutes, steam from the wet sheets began to fill the room. A half hour later, the sheets were dry. The monks, Dr. Benson believed, were able to perform this amazing feat by holding intensive visualizations after entering into a state of profound relaxation. They created changes in their physical environment – in this case, they raised their temperatures high enough to dry the wet, cold sheets.

It seems the **one quality all great achievers have possessed is the ability to imagine or visualize.** They first create or achieve success in their mind's eye. Maxwell Maltz in *PSYCHOCYBERNETICS* set forth the theory that "**what is held in the mind is what a person becomes**." Any image we vividly hold in our mind and can feel as real will actualize in our life. Lauren Bacall shared her opinion with this quote, "Imagination is the highest kite that one can fly."

True Life Example: Stan Klimek is a great Photographer. I personally know he won eight awards for his photographic talents in one year. He fascinated me with his mastery of the power of imagination. The day before each of his photographic shoots, he spent several hours visualizing in minute detail the entire shoot. He'd arrange the angle of the lights in his mind and see exactly the position of his models. When I say he imagined every detail, he really did. For example, he would consider the time of day and the effect the outside lighting would have. His ability to create the picture before he actually took it made it exactly as he wanted it.

True Life Example: Liu Chi Kung was a world-renowned Pianist in the 1950's. He had no piano to practice on while imprisoned for seven years during the Cultural Revolution in China. Yet when he resumed his concert, tour fans said he played better than ever. You probably ask how was this possible? "I rehearsed every piece I had ever played, note by note, in my mind," he explained.

We human beings have so much potential! Let's be aware, accept and expect this. Let's use our imaginations as a conduit for the inspiration of the Infinite. Let's look at life as if we are about to see something extraordinary. Let's listen as if we were to hear the most enlightening information.

Let's lift our hearts and minds into the heavens to grasp an idea and bring it down to earth to paint, to write, to turn into music, to dance, or... Let's turn the abstract into beautiful reality.

Case Study: Guided imagery is a way of using our imagination by focusing our attention on an inner, mental picture that we create. Per Dr. Jonathan Parker, "Guided imagery has been shown by research to lower blood pressure, reduce anxiety, depression and physical pain, reduce or eliminate habits, heighten immune functioning, ease nausea during chemotherapy, lower histamine responses and speed up recovery from cuts, burns, fractures and surgery. It also improves sports performance and some kinds of cognition." The power of our brain and our imagination is truly amazing!

How to Effectively Imagine

1. **List everything you want in life** with no limits or judgments. Just write down everything you want, whether you think you can get it, afford it or do it. Don't worry about prioritizing your wants. Just write, write, write. Just dream, dream, dream! If you want to win a Nobel peace prize, write it down. Don't worry about being too old, don't have the physical capability or don't have the money to do it. Just write it.
2. **Now, prioritize your wants and add details.**
3. **Relax**. The way to imagine is to first become deeply relaxed, yet awake. Eliminate any distractions. Let the tension in your muscles dissolve. Quiet your mind chatter. Perhaps play some soothing background music or listen to an audio that helps to create a state of relaxation. Breathe deeply with your eyes closed so you can create your own movie in your mind.
4. **Picture it**. Allow yourself to picture the desired outcome in as much detail as possible. Repeat this as often as possible. The repetition is important. Studies show in order to change a habit we need to practice the positive outcome we want for 21-to-30 days, without missing a day. The completeness of our imagery is very important so imagine the smallest details with as much clarity as possible.
5. **Feel yourself in the image** so that your subconscious accepts it as reality now. Actually, feel yourself in action in your picture.
6. **Hold those detailed images** in your mind to fuel your desires with passion into being! The vivid images you hold will take root in your life.

Our Subconscious Controls Us

Our subconscious mind actually controls us. It is because of our subconscious mind that we do so many things in our life without consciously thinking about them. It doesn't require our full concentration to breathe, walk or drive a car. Therefore, if the subconscious can control us, let's change it to be more positive and helpful to us.

Yes, in fact, we can change it. Repetition is a powerful way to accomplish this and, the most effective way, is to do the repetitions in your mind because in your mind you don't make any mistakes! ☺

True Life Example: Did you know you don't need an alarm clock to wake up? If you note what time it is when you go to sleep and what time you want to wake up, you will wake up at exactly that time. I do this all the time.

Our subconscious holds solutions for many of our concerns. Give your unanswered question to your subconscious as you fall asleep and you will most likely wake up with the answer.

Imagination Can Reshape the Future

Imagination is powerful. With imagination, we can reshape the future! Imagining with strong feeling we give positive input to that computer we call our brain - what we put in is what we get. **If we input detailed images with the positively charged feelings connected to them, we can change the world.**

Napoleon Hill inspired us with, "Cherish your visions and your dreams, as they are the children of your soul; the blueprints of your ultimate achievements." Using the wonder of imagination, you will live your happiest life.

Positive Expectation Statement™

For Happiness Action Tool™ #16
THE WONDER OF IMAGINATION

"I enhance my life with imagination."

(6 words)

For free gifts to support you in being your happiest, visit your happiness community at TheHappinessCommunity.com.

CHAPTER NINETEEN

Shake It Off and Step Up

HAPPINESS ACTION TOOL #17

The Asset of Perseverance

"Fall down seven times, get up eight."
~ Japanese proverb

"Patience and perseverance have a magical effect before which difficulties disappear and obstacles vanish."
~ John Quincy Adams

"Perseverance is a great element of success. If you only knock long enough at the gate, you are sure to wake up somebody."
~ Henry Wadsworth Longfellow

Perseverance is so powerful! Thomas Edison said, "Genius is one percent inspiration and ninety-nine percent perspiration." Therefore, one way to take responsibility for your best future is by sticking it out.

When faced with a challenge, don't give up. Believe you can do it and focus on the solution, sticking to it even though it may be difficult, knowing the outcome is worth the effort.

The keys to perseverance are commitment, patience and endurance. Slow and steady wins the race, so the expression goes. "Mountains DO Move ... One Stone at a Time!" exclaimed Rick Beneteau. People often give up just before they reach the goal line.

Charles Kettering shared with us, "Keep on going and the chances are you will stumble on something, perhaps when you least expect it. I have never heard of anyone stumbling on something sitting down."

SHAKE IT OFF AND STEP UP

There is a delightful poem by Edgar Albert Guest that begins:

> Somebody said that it couldn't be done,
> But he with a chuckle replied
> That "maybe it couldn't," but he would be one
> Who wouldn't say so till he'd tried.
> So he buckled right in with the trace of a grin
> On his face. If he worried he hid it.
> He started to sing as he tackled the thing
> That couldn't be done, and he did it.

True Life Example: This book is a story of perseverance. People often ask me how long it took to write it. The actual time spent writing it weighs in less heavily than the time I spent talking about it and sidestepping my destiny. It sat on a shelf ignored for way too many years.

Seeing a dream like this manifest awakened me even more to how good life really is, especially if we enjoy the day-to-day process of it. I spent another year re-writing, refining and striving for excellence. My passion fueled my perseverance and it became a real "labor of love." It proves that even if we do something in pieces we can accomplish it – kind of like eating an elephant. You do it one bite at a time. ☺

It is easier to stay persistent if we are doing something we feel strongly about. Linda Hancock Moore, this book's co-author, said, "One's ability to persevere is greatly enhanced by one's choice for that which they have passion."

Basketball player Michael Jordan shared, "I have missed more than nine thousand shots in my career. I have lost almost three hundred games. On twenty-six occasions, I have been entrusted to take the game winning shot – and I missed. And, I have failed over and over and over again in my life. And this is precisely why I succeed."

True Life Example: Most people have heard of the *CHICKEN SOUP FOR THE SOUL* book series, compiled by Jack Canfield and Mark Victor Hansen. Most people don't know more than a hundred publishers rejected their first book.

Mark and Jack refused to give up and I'll bet many of those publishers who rejected their book are sorry now. With over 100 million copies in print in 54 languages worldwide, *CHICKEN SOUP FOR THE SOUL* has made international publishing history. This is a great example of the asset of perseverance.

Most People Would Have Just Cried

Hoping for a different outcome yet doing the same things over and over, is one definition of "insanity." Napoleon Hill said, "The majority of men meet with failure because of their lack of persistence in creating new plans to take the place of those which fail."

Trust yourself when it comes to new ideas or changes, even if the new idea is to take a new direction. Stay open to new ideas and new opportunities. Just don't give up; you may find a way no one else thought of.

There is a story by an unknown author about a mule and perseverance. The story tells us what happened when the mule fell into the farmer's well. The story holds a lesson holds for all of us.

The farmer decided it wasn't worth the trouble to get him out of the well. Instead, he called his neighbors and enlisted them to bury the mule alive to put him out of his misery.

Yet, as they threw shovel after shovel full of dirt into the well the mule would just SHAKE IT OFF AND STEP UP. Soon he was able to step right over the wall and out of the well. You can read the entire parable at TheHappinessCommunity.com.

Most people would have just cried as the dirt hit them repeatedly. They wouldn't even consider there might be a solution. Don't let that happen to you. Keep an open mind and seek out new ways of doing things.

Did you know Thomas Edison tried ten thousand experiments before he figured out the formula for the light bulb! He kept at it with an open mind trying new approaches. In addition, he had to do it with the light available to him.☺

SHAKE IT OFF AND STEP UP

We learn the value of perseverance at an early age. Just because we make mistakes does not mean we have failed. We don't walk the first time we attempt to. We don't ride a bike perfectly the first time we attempt it. However, we keep at it and soon we have it mastered.

An unknown author said, "Babe Ruth hit more home runs than anyone; he also struck out more often than anyone."

How to Persevere

Perseverance by definition means steady persistence in adhering to a course of action, a belief, or a purpose, steadfastness, overcoming any disadvantages that stand in your way.

1. **Stick to it!**
2. **Set up a reward system for yourself**, if that will help.
3. **Stick to it!** ☺
4. **Stick to it!** ☺

Failure happens when you quit. Perseverance and failure cannot co-exist. Perseverance is the ultimate success insurance.

Sometimes it's Good to Quit

I feel it is important to add that the expression, "Quitters never win," is not always true. Sometimes quitting is the best thing we can do. It frees us to put our energy into something more appropriate for us.

Just make sure that before you throw in the towel you give it your best shot. Whether you are on a diet, hate your school, job or anything else; be sure to consider all options, as well as all consequences of quitting.

If you decide it is more beneficial for you to let it go, then give yourself permission to do so. Then you can get on with living your happiest life.

True Life Example: At one time as a part-time make-up artist, I had a number of clients who had been loyal for several years. I really enjoyed what I was doing and I still believe the products are exceptional. Once I began writing this book and was in touch with the joy of pursuing my mission in life I saw that it was time to look at this venture and see if it was time to let it go. I found myself feeling guilty for not spending more time and energy in marketing the business and following up with clients.

The decision I made was for it to be okay to do this as a fun side thing. I decided not to feel guilty for not keeping up with my clients. I would just let them come to me. If I lost some of them because of that, so be it.

I let myself joyfully approach the business, and guess what? Soon I had many old clients calling with re-orders as well as new clients calling me, too!

Many Famous People Had Handicaps

Sometimes it is not easy to be persistent. Still, if you believe in what you're doing, stick to it as best you can, even if it means suffering hardships, and you will eventually reap the rewards.

True Life Examples: Beethoven was deaf and Ray Charles was blind, as is musician Stevie Wonder. You may not know Thomas Edison, the inventor, and Albert Einstein, the scientist, had learning disabilities. The actor James Earl Jones stuttered.

Most people are aware that one of our best-known presidents, Franklin D. Roosevelt, was paralyzed and confined to a wheel chair due to his having polio. The artist, Vincent Van Gogh was mentally ill and Stephen Hawking, the physicist, had Lou Gehrig's disease.

Many famous people persevered despite having handicaps and disabilities and there are people who, even with what would seem overwhelming odds, have left a mark in history. You may not make a mark in the history books, yet each of us is a valuable part of life. Often we are unaware of how we contribute to the well-being of others. We often touch people and have no idea we have or how deeply.

Do your best and just stay at it. George Herbert Allen, American football coach and executive, said, "People of mediocre ability sometimes achieve outstanding success because they don't know when to quit."

SHAKE IT OFF AND STEP UP

Stick with your Happiness Action Tools™ and you're sure to learn the asset of perseverance in living your happiest life.

Positive Expectation Statement™

For Happiness Action Tool™ #17
THE ASSET OF PERSEVERANCE

"I keep at it until I get it"

(8 words)

For free gifts to support you in being your happiest, visit your happiness community at TheHappinessCommunity.com.

CHAPTER TWENTY

Become Different

HAPPINESS ACTION TOOL™ #18

The Insurance of Self-Development

*"Everyone thinks of changing the world,
but no one thinks of changing himself."*
~ Leo Tolstoy

*"He who asks a question is a fool for five minutes;
he who does not ask a question remains a fool forever."*
~ Chinese Proverb

"An investment in knowledge always pays the best interest."
~ Benjamin Franklin

Dr. Norman Vincent Peale told us, "If you want things to be different, perhaps the answer is to become different yourself." What an appropriate quote to begin this chapter.

If we want things to be different in our lives, we have to be different, and the way to do that is to develop ourselves – by finding new ways of doing things. Leo Buscaglia said, "Change is the end result of all true learning." Napoleon Hill put it this way, "If you do not conquer self, you will be conquered by self."

"Most, if not all, successful people are constant learners. They believe in life-long learning. Commit yourself to lifelong learning. The most valuable asset you'll ever have is your mind and what you put into it," explained Brian Tracy. He advised people to, "Invest three percent of your income in yourself (self-development) in order to guarantee your future."

Srully Blotnick believed that if you only had a certain amount of money to invest you should invest it in yourself. You can think of it this way: You pay only once for an education but you pay repeatedly for ignorance.

Nelson Mandela said, "Education is the most powerful weapon which you can use to change the world." Keep learning and expanding your mind so you can help change the world.

An unknown author said, "True abundance is co-creating one's reality with the grace of divine energy, and utterly without fear." We create our lives utilizing our Happiness Action Tools™. The fact that you are reading this book shows that you want to learn new ways of living your life. Keep up the good work!

Brian Tracy explained that, "The antidotes to fear and ignorance are desire and knowledge. Propel yourself forward by learning what you need to learn in order to do what you want to do."

Many Ways to Learn

There are so many ways available today to learn. We can learn by attending classes or lectures, teleseminars and webinars as well as going to school. We can read, whether that is by reading a physical book or via an electronic device such as our computer or an e-reader. We also have available to us: CD's, DVD's, videos, television, radio or other people.

So many exceptional people can teach us powerful and interesting things. Why not avail ourselves of their knowledge?

Here's a creative idea. Jim Rohn was a very effective personal development writer and speaker. He was one of the first people to introduce me to the idea of taking someone wiser or more learned to lunch or dinner. For the simple price of a meal, we can gain valuable information.

There Are Two Types of Education

James Truslow Adams explained that, "There are obviously two educations. One should teach us how to make a living and the other how to live."

It's not enough to get only a scholastic education. We also need what some people call "street smarts." We can learn so many things from other people and their experiences. Yet Douglas Adams pointed out, "Human beings, who are almost unique in having the ability to learn from the experience of others, are also remarkable for their apparent disinclination to do so."

We can also learn from our own experiences. Carol Burnett said, "I have always grown from my problems and challenges, from the things that don't work out, that's when I've really learned."

It's a good idea to pay attention as we go along. Ted W. Engstrom said, "We must expect to fail... but fail in a learning posture, determined not to repeat the mistakes, and to maximize the benefits from what is learned in the process."

Richard Bach said, "There are no mistakes. The events we bring upon ourselves, no matter how unpleasant, are necessary in order to learn what we need to learn; whatever steps we take, they're necessary to reach the places we've chosen to go."

John McEnroe said, "The important thing is to learn a lesson every time you lose. Life is a learning process and you have to try to learn what's best for you. Let me tell you, life is not fun when you're banging your head against a brick wall all the time."

Benjamin Franklin said, "Tell me and I forget. Teach me and I remember. Involve me and I learn." These words of wisdom remind us we need to put into action, or not, what we learn.

Friends of Our Mind

Dottie Walters was a lovely person, as well as being very successful professionally. She was an international speaker, an author, the President of Walters International Speakers Bureau and a founding member of The National Speakers' Association.

Her death in February 2007 saddened many people, as everyone thought well of her. To have attended her last marketing symposium and have the chance to sit and hold her hand, was a special blessing for me.

She often referred to her "friends of the mind." She said the shelves of the library are full of these friends and that she visited them often. Go to the library and make new friends soon, and often, or go buy a book and bring a friend home. Don't just do it for Dottie – do it for you! ☺

Learning Keeps Us Young

I really do love to learn. I am very curious. Maybe this is one reason I feel and appear younger than I am. ☺ Harvey Ullman said, "Anyone who stops learning is old, whether this happens at twenty or eighty. Anyone who keeps on learning not only remains young, but becomes constantly more valuable regardless of physical capacity."

Rosalyn S. Yakowk said the same thing in other words, "The excitement of learning separates youth from old age. As long as you're learning you're not old."

The famed actor Jack Nicholson believes strongly in the benefit of learning. He expressed, "The minute you're not learning I believe you're dead."

Celebrate Your Learning

Celebrate your learning. This will motivate you to learn more and therefore greatly expand your life. Set specific realistic goals for your learning and then celebrate those successes.

Abigail Adams said, "Learning is not attained by chance, it must be sought for with ardor and diligence." Decide to make learning a priority in your life.

Regularly utilize the Happiness Action Tool™ of self-development because as Jim Rohn shared with us, "Learning is the beginning of wealth. Learning is the beginning of health. Learning is the beginning of spirituality. Searching and learning is where the miracle process all begins."

Case Study: **Our brain is like a muscle and, as such, needs exercise daily for optimum strength and endurance.** In fact, scientists tell us there are steps we can take to forestall the inevitable consequences of aging, such as fogged memory and slowed wit. It may even be possible to prevent such conditions as Alzheimer's disease. Thank God scientists are always looking for ways for things to "become different."

BECOME DIFFERENT

Dr. Amir Sosas of Case Western Reserve University Medical School in Cleveland, said, "Read, read, read." He further said to do, "anything that stimulates the brain to think."

According to the *HEALING NEWSLETTER*, **"Scientists now know that the brain continually rewires and adapts itself, even in old age; large brain-cell growth continues into the teen years, and even the elderly can grown at least some new neurons."**

Reverend John Levy explained, "They say you can't teach new tricks to an old dog, but I believe you can, especially if the old dog stands to gain by learning the new trick."

Learn some new tricks. Exercise your brain and get what you want – and new neurons to boot!

Ideas for Self-Development

1. **Use any media as a learning tool**: classes, lectures, webinars, books, CD's, DVD's, videos, television, radio or other people.
2. **Use downtime to learn**. Be prepared for those unexpected downtimes by always having learning material with you.
3. **Record ideas**; your own and other people's. Keep a notebook, voice recorder or PDA with you at all times.
4. **Take someone wiser to lunch** and pick his/her brain.
5. **Listen for ideas** not matter where you are. Talk to strangers who may be next to you in line or on the elevator.
6. **Post good ideas where you will see them**. This might be inspirational quotes, a Positive Expectation Statement™ or a reminder of something to better you, maybe in picture form.

As B.B. King said, "The beautiful thing about learning is nobody can take it away from you." Shel Horowitz, best-selling author, expressed, **"Successful people have big libraries. So read to succeed."**

This quote by George Eliot is an especially good one to end this chapter: "It is never too late to be what we might have been."

Learning is discovery and expansion and can be the first step in changing any part of our life for the better. Utilizing the

BECOME DIFFERENT

Happiness Action Tool™ of self-development regularly will insure we are living our happiest life.

Positive Expectation Statement™

For Happiness Action Tool™ #18
THE INSURANCE OF SELF-DEVELOPMENT

"I now enjoy adding to my knowledge."

(7 words)

For free gifts to support you in being your happiest, visit your happiness community at TheHappinessCommunity.com.

CHAPTER TWENTY-ONE

No Man is an Island

HAPPINESS ACTION TOOL™ #19
THE ASSURANCE OF SUPPORT

"Treat people as if they were what they ought to be and you help them become what they are capable of being."
~ Johann Wolfgang von Goethe

"Love is blind; friendship closes its eyes."
~ English Proverb

"The only way to have a friend is to be one. A friend may well be reckoned the masterpiece of nature."
~ Ralph Waldo Emerson

We have other people in our lives because we need them. We need them to manufacture the products we use. We need them to provide the services we utilize. It would literally be a barren existence without the products and services provided by other people. We could never do everything ourselves, even though some of us do try. ☺

This famous quote by John Donne, says it well, "No man is an island, entire of itself. Every man is a piece of the continent, a part of the main if a clod be washed away by the sea, Europe is the less, as well as if a promontory were; as well as if a manor of thy friends or of thine own were; any man's death diminishes me, because I am involved in Mankind; and therefore never send to know for whom the bell tolls; it tolls for thee."

David J. Schwartz said, "Here is the basic rule for winning success. Let's mark it in the mind and remember it. The rule is: Success depends on the support of other people. The only hurdle between you and what you want to be is in the support of other people."

The people we have in our lives because we *choose to* are the most important because they contribute greatly to our health and well-being. It is these people who give our lives meaning, who acknowledge us as being special, and validate our existence. We look to them for support, encouragement and inspiration, and even advice on our decisions. These relationships support our enthusiasm and dreams so we need to carefully, lovingly nurture them.

Frank A. Clark shared these appropriate words, "A baby is born with a need to be loved and never outgrows it." Dr. Charmaine Griffiths said, "This growing body of **research only goes to highlight how important social support is for everyone**, not just those in a relationship."

Those of us with many friends to turn to, and enjoy, seem to be the happiest people. People who focus on themselves and their faults – how they look and how they measure up – are the unhappiest. Whether we are attractive or are not, it's not about how we look. **It's how we *feel* about how we look.** Feeling unattractive causes us to focus on our self and our imperfections. I can't say for sure, yet I will guess you don't enjoy being around negative people either.

Admiration is Like Catnip

Let the people you admire and respect know how you feel about them. Admiration is like catnip to almost anyone.

Richard Bach, in his book, *ILLUSIONS,* pointed out, "The bond that links your true family is not one of blood, but of respect and joy in each other's life. Rarely do members of one's family grow up under the same roof." Of course, he was referring to the extended families we create because we choose to have them as our family. He also says, "Your friends will know you better in the first minutes you meet than your acquaintances will know you in a thousand years."

Love from friends and family is a precious gift. As Eleanor Roosevelt realized, "Many people will walk in and out of your life, but only true friends will leave a footprint in your heart." Anais

Nin said, "Each friend represents a world in us, a world possibly not born until they arrive, and it is only by this meeting that a new world is born."

There's a French saying that expresses this well, "Treasures are not friends, but a friend is a treasure." Nurture and protect that treasure. Be willing to give time and energy to that treasure to keep it shining and bright. The best way to keep a friendship intact is to never take it for granted; to consistently acknowledge the beauty of it – and the qualities of the friend who is a co-partner in its' creation and maintenance.

Bonaro W. Overstreet said, "If I can line up the people who, back through the ages, have gone at life in ways I greatly admire, then I can feel their strength supporting me, all their standards and values pointing the way in which I am to go."

Life is more enjoyable and rewarding when we have a deep level of personal and professional friendship. How lucky we are to have people in our lives who stick by us. How blessed we are to have good friends and loved ones.

Be Cautious Though

Do be cautious about whom you trust and spend your precious time with. We've discussed this in other chapters, yet it's worth repeating a second time. Do the people in your life drain you or energize you?

It is important to make every effort to have only those who energize us in our lives, for as Patricia Lynn Reilly said, "Certain activities, attitudes, foods, and persons support the cultivation of an unconscious life. They draw us away from our center. They throw us off-balance. They deplete the soul."

Return the Favor

Do you know what the word reciprocity means? It's one of my favorite words. Webster defines it as "mutual action and reaction." It is "in-kind positive or negative responses of individuals towards the actions of others," according to Wikipedia's ever-evolving information. It is NOT about keeping score. Simply, it is returning a favor: You do something for me and I do something for you. It is a win-win situation.

So, remain loyal to those people who are supportive of you through the highs and lows of your life. Look at who is supporting you in your life, especially during your challenging times. Be warm and genuine in your acknowledgements to those people who have offered you their services, support and loyalty. Michael Jordan put it like this, "Talent wins games, but teamwork wins championships."

Besides, helping others helps us because it brings us the joy of generosity. However, doing something for someone else hoping for a selfish outcome will never match the joy of giving something to someone with no expectation attached. Still, **giving love and helping others is definitely a great way to achieve happiness**. Brian Tracy reminds us, "Everything that you do or say that raises the self-esteem of another raises yours as well."

Supporting others we support ourselves. However ultimately, self-satisfaction achieved with a selfish motive is momentary and false, leading to disappointment. When was the last time you gave an unexpected gift to someone? Remember how excited you were at just the thought of the look of joy on the recipient's face? Who's the recipient of your next gift? ☺

I like what Norman Vincent Peale said about supporting others. He said, "Joy increases as you give it, and diminishes as you try to keep it for yourself. In giving it, you will accumulate a deposit of joy greater than you ever believed possible."

In *LIFE'S GOLDEN TICKET* Brendon Burchard wrote, "You see, most people, maybe including you, have lived life as if they were at the whim of circumstance and as if they were supposed to get something from the world. The miracle makers in this world, though, are the people who **live by choice** and **live to contribute**. They ask what they're making happen, and they ask what they're giving. I think you've probably learned a lot... My final lesson to you, then, is about contribution, and it says simply this: if you want your life experiences to be bright, choose to contribute."

Six Hugs a Day

A hug has a healing effect on both our bodies and our emotions and helps keep our immune systems strong. "For human beings, you need two hugs a day to survive, four hugs for maintenance, six hugs to grow," said Virginia Satir. I've heard others say that ought to be doubled. We all benefit from feeling loved and special and hugs are an easy way to accomplish this. ☺

Let's support each other and see if we can outdo those numbers. It will be fun giving those hugs (and getting them returned!) and it will help us stay healthier. I predict you will get warm response to a simple, "Can I have a hug?" Yes, I am suggesting we show our vulnerability and let others know we need their support. Dave Lakani, "Mr. Persuasion," pointed out that, "People won't know you need love unless you tell them."

Share Your Pain and Your Joy

When we share our sorrow with a friend, it can help lessen our pain. Some people consider it a weakness to ask for support if things are not going perfectly in their lives. "Asking for help doesn't mean we are weak or incompetent. It usually indicates an advanced level of honesty and intelligence," expressed Anne Wilson Schaef.

According to a Swedish proverb, "Shared joy is a double joy; shared sorrow is half a sorrow." A Latin proverb says, "Of no worldly good can the joy be perfect, unless it is shared by a friend." Isn't sharing your news with someone the first thing you want to do when something good happens to you?

Share Your Dreams with Only a Select Few

Share your dreams with a few people who will help you achieve them. They will support and encourage you when the going gets tough, as life occasionally does throw up a few roadblocks along the way. Richard De Vos said, "Few things in the world are more powerful than a positive push – a smile. A word of optimism and hope, a 'you can do it!' when things are rough."

Be generous in supporting others in their dreams, too. Dr. Wayne Dyer said, "Love is the ability and willingness to allow those that you care for to be what they choose for themselves without any insistence that they satisfy you." Realize that when people don't support you they are either, not truly your friend or, they are just not in a good emotional state in their life to be able to share your joy. As Jeffrey Gitomer shared, "People try to rain on your parade because they have no parade of their own."

Listening Can Be the Best Support

Walter Anderson said, "Good listeners, like precious gems, are to be treasured." We discussed the wonderful action of listening before. It's just so worth repeating because as Paul Tillich said, "The first duty of love is to listen."

Have you ever noticed someone you thought was fascinating actually shared very little with you about who he or she is, or what was happening in his or her life? They, instead, spent the majority of the time listening to you! Develop that same wise skill for yourself, from your strongest place of consideration and true empathy. Learn to listen and the whole world will draw near to you and want to know what you have to say.

Listen with your heart as well as your ears. Look into the face of the speaker, so we don't miss those "unspoken" but heartfelt pieces of the conversation, and when you get distracted, mark your place so upon return you can bring it back with a sincere and thoughtful, "and you were saying?" Very often, you will be blessed in hearing so much more than just what is being said.

True Life Example: Linda, our Co-author, shared the following story to explain how she learned the value of just listening:

> I loved my mother and father, even though they divorced when I was four, and as the line goes in the movie, ***Hope Floats***, "I spent my whole life getting over it," my childhood that is.
>
> Having survived it though, I also, like many young adults, began to believe that I had become more sophisticated than my parents, and

certainly much smarter. At some point, I think I even started thinking they had nothing left to teach me, and with that, I think I may have quit really listening. At the age of thirty-three, and about to make one of the worst decisions of my life, moving from Texas to New York, I decided to first visit my mother.

A hard- working, good hearted woman, she was always busying herself with selfless things, always on her feet cooking and asking if she could do anything for me, always full of happy chatter, chatter full of every little simple thing that gave her days meaning. Half-listening I could feel the nagging inside of me over the decision I was making. Half-listening I could feel the love I had for my mother and the reasons I had needed to visit, but most of what she was saying, I was not hearing.

Then as the evening wore on, she stopped as she always did, with the chatter, and begin to just listen, while I on the on the other hand pontificated tirelessly; about my new boy friend, my new clothes, my new half-baked exciting plan, and all my new found philosophies. On this particular evening, for some reason, I suddenly noticed. "Oh, I'm sorry," I said, and I will never forget the next words that came from my mouth, "You probably have not understood a word I've said."

The only hope any of us have in growing is to be aware of our mistakes and our need for growth. I can tell you in that moment, hearing those words come from my mouth, I was suddenly aware.

What my mother said next though was even more compelling. She said in a soft respectful tone, "I may not always understand what you have to say, but I always want to hear what you have to say."

To this day I don't know which was more amazing; what she said to me, or the thought that I might have missed knowing the depth of my mother had I not stopped in that moment and allowed her to say what she had to say. Now I know how much I had missed, all those years, by only half listening to her loving chatter.

Listen Actively

Linda's story reflects the opinion of K. Thomas Finley of Mental Dynamics who said, "To be an effective listener, you must be interested in what is being said. This means you must abandon your prejudices about certain subjects, then make a special effort to listen and listen aggressively... Look for something of real value to you in all speeches and discussions. You will usually find it. Also, ask questions. Pretend you are interested – and soon you will be."

How to Be a Great Listener

Some come to us with a need to "vent" distress, while others need a reply. Everyone has a story he or she wants to share. No matter what their reason for needing us to listen, listening is a gift that keeps on giving, and gives back to the giver.

1. **Practice listening**. Focus on what the other person is saying without interrupting and telling your story.
2. **Avoid jumping ahead** to what you think is the end of the sentence, or worse, the end of the story. You will rob the conversation of surprise, or make it your story, not theirs.
3. **Stay tuned in** to what the person is saying. If you're interrupted, you will know where the story left off. (This could be a test.☺)
4. **Don't evaluate or judge**, however listen for the unspoken.
5. **Ask sincere questions** to show you care. Questions are often more effective because they sound less like judgment.
6. **Never rush or interrupt** the speaker; it is a dead giveaway that you may not really want to listen.☹
7. **Remember every speaker is important** and has their story to tell. Even a story you think you've heard before will be different, maybe closer to the truth, or more interesting.

Helen Steiner Rice expressed, "When you ask God for a gift, be thankful if he sends, not diamonds, pearls or riches, but the love of real, true friends." Assure yourself a happy life with the support of family and friends.

Positive Expectation Statement™

For Happiness Action Tool™ #19
THE ASSURANCE OF SUPPORT

"I surround myself with positive people."

(6 words)

CHAPTER TWENTY-TWO

"Dance like Nobody's Watching"

HAPPINESS ACTION TOOL™ #20

THE MERIT OF ENTHUSIASM

"Nobody grows old merely by living a number of years.
We grow old by deserting our ideals.
Years may wrinkle the skin,
but to give up enthusiasm wrinkles the soul."
~ Samuel Ullman

"We act as though comfort and luxury were
the chief requirements of life,
when all that we need to make us really happy
is something to be enthusiastic about."
~ Charles Kingsley

"Vigor is contagious, and whatever makes us either think or feel strongly
adds to our power and enlarges our field of action."
~ Ralph Waldo Emerson

Enthusiasm is when we feel like jumping up and down and screaming, "Yes!" We are so very alive when we approach life with enthusiasm, which insures life will greet us with enthusiasm, and we will get the most from it.

Poet Maya Angelou said, "Life loves to be taken by the lapel and told, 'I'm with you kid. Let's go!'" At 83, Mavis Leyrer said, "Life's journey is not to arrive at the grave safely, in a well preserved body, but rather to skid in sideways, totally worn out, shouting, 'Wow! What a ride!'"

Norman Vincent Peale told us, "If you have zest and enthusiasm you attract zest and enthusiasm. Life does give back in kind." He went on to say, **"Life's blows cannot break a person whose spirit is warmed at the fire of enthusiasm."**

George Bernard Shaw wrote, "Life is no brief candle to me. It is sort of a splendid torch which I have got hold of for a moment, and I want to make it burn as brightly as possible before handing it on to future generations."

Curiosity Breed Enthusiasm

Eduora Welty suggests we, "Give curiosity freedom." I second that idea! When we are curious we have enthusiasm to satisfy that curiosity, which is why I say curiosity breeds enthusiasm.

Betty Smith advised us to, "Look at everything as though you were seeing it either for the first or last time. Then your time on earth will be filled with glory."

Eleanor Roosevelt, explained it like this, "I think, at a child's birth, if a mother could ask a fairy godmother to endow it with the most useful gift, that gift would be curiosity."

Boredom is a Sin

Dale Carnegie asked, "Are you bored with life? Then throw yourself into some work you believe in with all your heart, live for it, die for it, and you will find happiness that you thought could never be yours." I can't imagine ever being bored with life.

True Life Example: My friend, Tod Spence, believes, "If there is a sin, it is that of being bored." There are so many things to do, see and learn in life. I have so many projects that my biggest problem is in deciding which one to focus on.

William Feather shared "No person is a failure who is enjoying life." Samuel Goldwyn said, "No person who is enthusiastic about his work has anything to fear from life. All the opportunities in the world are waiting to be grasped by people who are in love with what they are doing."

Enthusiasm Keeps Us Young

Young people are naturally enthusiastic. It makes sense that if we keep our enthusiasm we keep our youth. So, "Go for it!" Whatever it is, I say go for it joyfully and enthusiastically! You will reap so much.

"DANCE LIKE NOBODY'S WATCHING"

Enthusiastic people throw themselves into their projects; they give it their all. Like a child, they are eager and curious. Aldus Huxley said, "The genius of life is to carry the spirit of childhood into old age."

Norman Vincent Peale shared this thought, "Those who are fired with an enthusiastic idea and who allow it to take hold and dominate their thoughts find that new worlds open for them. As long as enthusiasm holds out, so will opportunities." Find your passions and live them; live them enthusiastically.
Mark Twain shared this famous expression, "Dance like nobody's watching; love like you've never been hurt. Sing like nobody's listening; live like it's heaven on earth."

William Arthur Ward said, "Enthusiasm is the match that lights the candle of achievement." Enthusiasm helps us hang in there when the going gets tough. Enthusiastic people love what they do and are not concerned about money, power or title.

Henry Ford emphatically said, "Enthusiasm is at the bottom of all progress! With it, there is accomplishment; without it, there are only alibis." Mary Kay Ash expressed, "A mediocre idea that generates enthusiasm will go further than a great idea that inspires no one."

It's often the little things in life that add up to being the big things. So, be enthusiastic about even the small things. Dale Carnegie said it well, "Don't be afraid to give your best to what seemingly are small jobs. Every time you conquer one it makes you that much stronger. If you do the little jobs well, the big ones will tend to take care of themselves."

Enthusiasm is Contagious

Enthusiasm is contagious. Enthusiasm excites others, causing them to join us in our enthusiasm. **Passion for life draws people to us like a magnet.** It can turn strangers into friends. One of the easiest ways to increase your enthusiasm and passion is to surround yourself with people who exhibit these same attributes.

"DANCE LIKE NOBODY'S WATCHING"

True Life Example: The most effective way to become enthusiastic is to act enthusiastic. This may seem too you like you are pretending, and in a way, you are. Yet, before you know it, you will actually feel enthusiastic – and may even feel like dancing. ☺

I was out with my friend, Marisa Stewart, and I got to see the merit of enthusiasm in action. We were attending a concert at the pier in Santa Monica, California featuring legendary guitarist Dick Dale. We found a parking space up close, which started an evening of Marisa being enthusiastic and grateful. All evening she repeated, "What a perfect evening. This is so much fun!"

I was not at my most energetic that evening, yet I did not want to "rain on her parade," so I acted enthusiastic and soon I was feeling it. Enthusiasm is definitely contagious. People really do love to be around happy enthusiastic people. People were attracted to us all evening long. She was right; it was a perfect evening and so much fun. A lot of it was her fault – it was because of her sincere enthusiasm.

With enthusiasm, we live life wholeheartedly and take pleasure in the smallest things. We feel the joy of childhood again with a twinkle in our eye. This is probably why we all enjoy being around children – their joy is contagious!

Leo Buscaglia lived his life wholeheartedly enthusiastic, "I still get wildly enthusiastic about little things... I play with leaves. I skip down the street and run against the wind," he told us.

Even the respected Sir Winston Churchill believed in the power of enthusiasm. He said, "Success is going from failure to failure without a loss of enthusiasm."

No matter what your rational mind says, find out what makes your heart soar. Find out what makes you enthusiastic. Make a commitment to yourself to do those things that keep you enthusiastic and happy.

Because, as Leo Buscaglia exclaimed, "Life is a paradise for those who love many things with a passion." Anita Roddick put it like this, "To succeed you have to believe in something with such a passion that it becomes a reality."

"Every memorable act in the history of the world is a triumph of enthusiasm. Nothing great was ever achieved without enthusiasm because it gives any challenge or any occupation, no matter how frightening or difficult, a new meaning. Without enthusiasm we are doomed to a life of mediocrity but with it we can accomplish miracles," Og Mandino shared.

William Ellis expressed, "If you want to be enthusiastic, act enthusiastic. Then inner enthusiasm will follow." We can create enthusiasm from the tiniest spark of kindness, good humor, generosity, or willingness and it is ultimately contagious, not to mention more attractive.☺

How to Be Enthusiastic

In the family of emotions, enthusiasm must be the first cousin to passion, and if not coming spontaneously, can, with enough of it, start to make an endeavor feel like it's coming from passion. If enthusiasm is not there from the start, "act as if" it is and fuel it!

1. **Breathe deeply and smile**, whether you feel like it or not.
2. **Stir up interest by activating your curiosity** in the endeavor. The more you know about it, the more interested you will become.
3. **Create excitement and make it fun**. You can turn many boring tasks into games. One little boy, when asked to wash the dishes, made a game of seeing how high he could stack them.☺

Go forth in life with enthusiasm. Grab the gusto. You'll naturally live your happiest life with this Happiness Tool™.

Positive Expectation Statement™

For Happiness Action Tool™ #20
THE MERIT OF ENTHUSIASM

"I seize the day with enthusiasm."

(6 words)

For free gifts to support you in being your happiest, visit your happiness community at TheHappinessCommunity.com.

CHAPTER TWENTY-THREE

Do Some Internal Jogging

HAPPINESS ACTION TOOL™ #21

THE TREASURE OF PLAY

"God hath made me laugh, so that all that hear will laugh with me."
~ Genesis 91:6

"A person without a sense of humor is like a wagon without springs – jolted by every pebble in the road."
~ Henry Ward Beecher

"Mix a little foolishness with your serious plans: it's lovely to be silly at the right moment."
~ Horace

When all else fails we can laugh. Laughter! Oh blessed laughter! Is there anything more healing? Is there anything more energizing? As I said, when all else fails LAUGH! **Why laugh? It's been said, "Laughter triggers joy."**

William James said, "We don't laugh because we're happy, we're happy because we laugh." The famed entertainer Bill Cosby said, "You can turn painful situations around through laughter. If you can find humor in anything, even poverty, you can survive it."

Reverend Billy Graham encouraged us with these words, "A keen sense of humor helps us to overlook the unbecoming, understand the unconventional, tolerate the unpleasant, overcome the unexpected, and outlast the unbearable."

Red Skelton was my mother's favorite comedian. He shared these wise words, "I live by this credo: Have a little laugh at life and look around you for happiness instead of sadness. Laughter has always brought me out of unhappy situations. Even in your darkest moment, you usually can find something to laugh about if you try hard enough."

DO SOME INTERNAL JOGGING

Case Study: The ability to laugh at ourselves or to find joy when everything around us seems to be falling apart is a valuable resource for improving or maintaining our good health.

An increasing number of scientific studies are indicating laughter may help ward off illness, boost the immune system and stimulate major bodily functions. It seems laughter is a natural stress reliever. It increases oxygen, stamina and our breathing capacity. Medical journals are full of reasons to laugh for the health of it.

An unknown author said, "Meet the challenge of life with laughter. Learn laughter from little children; develop a playful attitude toward problems. Use laughter as a safety valve to keep yourself sane and relaxed. Remember the old proverb: 'A little nonsense now and then is relished by the wisest men.' Most of all learn to laugh at yourself; meet each day with a sense of humor. Laughter is the best medicine for a long and happy life."

This really ought to be a chapter on balance. You've heard the old proverb, "All work and no play makes Jack a dull boy." Too bad that isn't true just for Jack – it's true for all of us.

There is wisdom in Ann Smith's words, "The more balanced our lives, the more serene we feel." William A. Ward expressed, "A well-developed sense of humor is the pole that adds balance to your steps as you walk the tightrope of life."

Find a balance between work, play and other activities. **Often, play ends up as our last priority. Yet, I really believe we need to make it a high priority in our lives on a regular basis – ideally daily,** because as Phyllis Diller put it, "A smile is a curve that sets everything straight." I like Silver Rose's attitude, she said, "Adults made up work as an excuse to play together." That sure puts a new twist on work, doesn't it?

True Life Example: I have a friend, who's really funny, but who says sadly she's a "grinner, not a laugher." She says she loves to make people laugh, not only because she loves people and believes laughter heals, but she always hopes that if she surrounds herself with laughter, she'll have a chance to "catch the wave." She's also the friend we have to remind to "breathe."

Both laughter and breathing seem to be connected to the ability to just "let go," to give up the egotistical notion that one is responsible for so much that is really out of our control. (I've heard her catch that wave, by the way, breathing deeply; her laughter spilling out into the other laughter and into the world. It's literally music to the ears!) I'm making a note now to suggest she use this special Positive Expectation Statement™, "I am enjoying the breath of laughter!"

No Matter How Old We Are We All Need to Play

Case Study: Children laugh on the average 400 times per day. The average adult laughs only 15 times a day. Wow! What a difference. Yet, many adults would tell you their favorite sound is of children laughing. Let's consciously close that gap! No wonder we adults get what Joel Goodman calls "hardening of the attitudes." As he said, "Humor is a wonderful way to prevent a hardening of the attitudes!"

True Life Example: Robert Fisher, a well-known comedy writer, for such greats as Groucho Marx, Bob Hope, Red Skelton, George Burns, Jack Benny, Fanny Brice, Alan King and Lucille Ball, was escorted to one of my birthday parties by my THEN "laughing impaired" friend and now co-author, Linda Hancock Moore. She had met him at a speaking engagement of his, praising the power of laughter. He had strongly suggested that if you had not had a good laugh that day, you should start thinking about something funny, just so you could stir one up, and failing that, make one up!

Have you heard about *LAUGHTER YOGA* yet? It's an organization started by Dr. Madan Kataria, an Indian doctor and student of Yoga. The website, LaughterYoga.org, tells how he was convinced of the medical benefits of laughter and Yogic breathing exercises, and was searching for a way to bring these benefits to modern man. Per the website, "Thanks to Dr. Kataria countless people all over the world today enjoy the benefits of a daily dose of laughter practicing *LAUGHTER YOGA* at laughter clubs or at their workplace."

The premise of *LAUGHTER YOGA* is that laughter exercises, which start with "faking" a laugh, usually lead to real laughter, especially when practiced in a group. Sessions include being lead through a series of exercises that each elicit laughter. *Laughter Yoga* sessions are held worldwide. I attended a class and it was so much fun!

The website LaughterYoga.org claims, "A regular 20 minute laughter session can have a profound impact on our health and well-being." It goes on to say, "When we laugh our bodies release a cocktail of hormones and chemicals that have startling positive effects on our system. Stress is reduced, blood pressure drops, depression is lifted, your immune system is boosted and more. Western science is just starting to discover the great effects of laughter."

True Life Example: I've mentioned my "adopted Mother," Alice. I gave her an orange postcard that read, "We don't stop playing because we grow old, we grow old because we stop playing." That fit her so well. She was so youthful. She loved to kindly tease people. She loved that postcard; it was not especially attractive, but it never left the shelf in her family room. I'm sure she agreed with Mary Pettibone Poole, "He who laughs, lasts!" Alice was 86 when she died from a brain tumor. Up until then she was active, vibrant and playful with full mental capacity.

Life is better if it is in balance. So, take time to relax and play. You will find you truly perform better in all areas of your life. Looking at life's challenges from the lighter side allows us to see things with better perspective. There is usually humor in every situation. We just need to make the effort to see it. Sir Francis Bacon shared his opinion, "Imagination was given to man to compensate him for what he isn't, and a sense of humor to console him for what he is." Anne Wilson Schaef shared, "Laughter is like the human body wagging its tail."

Laughter is Internal Jogging

Case Study: Dr. William F. Fry, Jr., then Clinical Psychiatry Professor at Stanford University Medical School, and a Lifetime Achievement Award Recipient, as well as a recognized pioneer documenting the physiological effects of laugher said, "I'm sure that laughter plays a major role in keeping us healthy. **There's hardly a system in the body, even major bodily functions, that a hearty laugh doesn't stimulate.** The respiratory, cardiovascular, muscular, endocrine and central nervous systems are stimulated when you laugh; and the chest, thorax and abdominal muscles, contract along with the diaphragm, heart, lungs and liver." *[Emphasis added.]*

Dr. Fry described **laughter as a type of internal jogging**, "Your heart rate can double within a very short period of time and oxygen consumption is increased. After you're done laughing, there is a decrease in heart rate, promoting relaxation. Increased cardiovascular activity during laughter is accompanied by a rise in blood pressure, resulting in increased circulation." **Laughing 100 times a day is equivalent to approximately 10 minutes of hard rowing or riding a stationary bike for 15 minutes.**

Dr. Fry identified a number of potential benefits of laughter, which include a stronger immune system, better and easier breathing and a lessening of pain perception. "It's about time that humor not be considered a trivial and inconsequential part of our lives, but is in fact vital in terms of health and interaction... And, here's the beautiful part: You don't need equipment, you don't need a nice day, you don't need humor."

He revealed that even faking merriment has a positive physiological effect! "I asked some of the subjects merely to pretend they were laughing at something funny, and I observed the same cardiovascular benefits, including exercise of the respiratory muscles, as in genuine laughter," he explained. Try laughing right now and feel your muscles tighten.

That's right, even a phony smile may be good for you. Most certainly, it will be when it becomes real. Several studies show that changing facial expressions, either for real or simulated, can change a person's mood. It's widely accepted that a smile makes people happier and a frown seems to make them sadder. Therefore, it seems to be a logical conclusion that all we need to do to be happier is to smile, and even better, laugh!

Laughter Really is the Best Medicine

Scientists have discovered the human brain produces endorphins and encephalin, secretions with morphine-like molecules. These chemicals provide the body with its own pain-reducing substance. Laughter can act to stimulate production of these chemicals. Just as negative emotions can compromise the immune system, positive emotions and laughter can help strengthen the immune system.

Case Study: In a research study, conducted at Eastern New England College in Massachusetts, two groups viewed either *RICHARD PRYOR LIVE* or an educational film. The results showed that the humor group tested higher for an antibody that decreased the incidence of upper respiratory illnesses.

A study at Loma Linda University showed, **thirty minutes after 20 medical students laughed through a comedy video, their disease fighting white blood cells increased by 25%.** "If we took what we now know about laughter and bottled it, it would require FDA approval," said Dr. Lee S. Berk, PH CHES FACSM, leader of the laughter study and Assistant Professor of Pathology at Loma Linda's School of Medicine at the time of the study. *[Emphasis added.]*

Case Study: In 2002, Researchers at the University of California at Irvine reported even looking forward to something funny can contribute to physiological effects that reduce stress. The research team led by Dr. Berk presented its findings at a meeting of the Society for Neuroscience. The research involved sixteen subjects at California's Loma Linda University. Eight knew in three days they would be watching a funny movie and **just knowing they were going to be watching a funny video, experienced decreases in the levels of three stress hormones and increases in stress-reducing endorphins**

and growth hormones. Dr. Berk explained that mood and body changes persist well after experiencing actual funny events - suggesting that optimism helps people recover from illness and "supporting the reality that there may be biology to the concept of hope."

Case Study: Matt Weinstein, Ph.D. believed good, honest, noncompetitive, let-your-hair-down fun is essential for everyone's good health. He noted, "The problem with adults is that they lose the ability to play. We do most of our playing – using the right brain [the right hemisphere is the artistic/creative center] – in the first five years of life. Then we go to school and learn the power of the left-brain [the analytical/learning center]. The problem is that we leave the right brain totally behind. People are not by nature depressed or bored, yet everyone on this planet gets that way. To me, boredom is a form of slow death... Too much stress and workaholism causes people to become ill. Play is really essential to stress reduction."

Case Study: Many doctors believe laughter and play are important in combating illness. O. Carl Simonton revealed that, "The first thing a person does when he finds out he's ill is stop playing. It shouldn't be that way. Play is mandatory, not elective. Playing is an activity that tends to produce emotions of joy and the experience of having fun. Feeling joyful and feeling like having fun increases our energy. Playing also mobilizes our desire to live because life becomes more meaningful."

Anger Has the Opposite Effect

Case Study: Anger has the opposite effect to humor leading to the squeezing of blood vessels and heart disease. A Duke University study found **hostile people are 4 to 7 times more likely to be dead by age 50** than those who are not hostile. Anger *is* a natural emotion, one we ought not to feel guilty about having when it is justified, however, in most instances, it would be better to do everything possible to intelligently, and fairly, "disarm" it.

Laughter, on the other hand, is good for us as it "pumps the heart and the muscles of the abdomen, chest, shoulder, and neck, stimulates our brains, ventilates our lungs, and raises our heart rates, blood pressure, respiration, and circulation. **It's a total body experience,**" teaches Dr. Fry.

We'll Live Longer if We Smile

Case Study: Optimists live longer! On average pessimists die 19% earlier *than their expected life spans*. Doctors at the Mayo Clinic in Rochester, Minnesota gave 800 adults personality tests in the mid 1960's and determined 15% were optimists, 15% pessimists and the rest were in between. Their death rates were compared with their test outcomes thirty years later. "The link between mind and body is real. Outlook really does matter," said Toshihiko Maruta, M.D., Professor of Psychiatry at the Mayo Clinic.

Psychologist Dr. Annette Goodheart, stated, "Humor helps an individual confront personal problems in a more relaxed and creative state. I think laughter is a perfect kind of self-help tool. I use it as a process for healing, as a pain-killer and for helping patients gain a perspective on illness and problems."

True Life Example: Many hospitals have humor and clown programs. There are special channels on in-room television sets so patients can enjoy comedy films at any hour of the day or night. A special brightly decorated room called the LIVING ROOM, has easy chairs, a humor library and media equipment at a Texas hospital. Duke University Medical Center has the LAUGH MOBILE, a gaily-decorated cart loaded with humorous books, games, etc.

In New York City, Clown's Care Unit includes clowns who visit many area hospitals each week, maintain a regular schedule of home visits and participate in community events. They draw blood with red crayons, examine funny bones, and cheer up patients with tricks, gags and giggles. Reverend Mark Bredholt, chaplain for hospice and oncology services at Baptist Medical Center in Columbia, South Carolina, began a clown program with a handful of self-made clowns and a lot of enthusiasm.

Patients have responded positively to the clown visits. Reverend Bredholt shared his belief that clowns have a very special place in our culture, "There's a lot about a clown that is a lot about humanity. The word 'clown' is derived from 'clod', which is a clump of dirt. The Hebrew poetry of Genesis tells us that God took a clump of dirt and breathed life into it creating the first man, Adam. Clowns are very much a part of humanity and all that it represents."

Case Study: Former editor of the *SATURDAY REVIEW*, Dr. Norman Cousins, was also Adjunct Professor at the UCLA School of Medicine. His book, *ANATOMY OF AN ILLNESS*, had a tremendous impact on the laughter-health connection. He overcame a serious degenerative illness by taking an active role in his own recovery. Dr. Cousins incorporated all kinds of positive emotions into his treatment, including love, hope, faith, a will to live, festivity, purpose and determination with laughter figuring prominently. A nurse read to him from humorous books. He also watched funny movies.

His experiment worked, "I made the joyous discovery that **10 minutes of genuine belly laughter had an anesthetic effect and would give me at least two hours of pain-free sleep**. When the painkilling effect of the laughter wore off, we would switch on the motion-picture projector again, and not infrequently, it would lead to another pain-free sleep interval." Dr. Cousins' prognosis had been "death." Yet, **using his techniques he did what no one thought was possible; he lived another 30 years**. *[Emphasis added.]*

Laughter Can't Hurt

A few recommendations for using humor to strengthen us include seeing our life as a sitcom, sharing humor with others and starting the day with laughter. Another idea is to set aside an evening for humor. Also, laugh just for its' own sake!

Case Study: It's a good idea to avoid that killer called anger. **Your risk of a heart attack is 2.3 times greater for the next two hours after being angry** according to a study of

1,623 people by Deaconess Hospital for the Prevention of Cardiovascular Disease. Try humor and laughter to cure anger!

It's certain; play and laughter can't hurt. **There are no documented negative side effects from laughter**, except of course the occasional sore stomach if we overdo it. Humor and laughter can reduce stress, ease pain, foster recovery and brighten our outlook on life. So, if your doctor tells you to lighten up, do as he says! ☺

Remember, "We don't stop playing because we grow old, we grow old because we stop playing?" Keep yourself young doing something fun every day and something especially fun on your day off. (You do take at least one day a week off, don't you?! ☺)

You might want to smile when no one else is around because as Andy Rooney put it, "If you smile when no one else is around, you really mean it." Warren Miller smiled, "Don't take life seriously, because you can't come out of it alive." Moreover, as Doug Hort shared, "Smile, it's free therapy." ☺

How to Play

Ah, come on, do we really have to give you ideas for this one? Just go do something fun that makes you smile, if not laugh out loud! ☺ And, repeat regularly!

Life is Fragile and Brief

I found a greeting card not long after my mother died that touched me deeply. It said, "Life is fragile and brief. So, do what makes you happy." Give yourself permission to play, smile and laugh. You will find the treasure of your happiest life with this significant, yet easy and fun Happiness Action Tool™.

Positive Expectation Statement™

For Happiness Action Tool™ #21
THE TREASURE OF PLAY

"I enjoy the treasure of play."

(6 words)

PART 3

Maintenance

CHAPTER TWENTY-FOUR

Staying Happy

SUMMARY

"What the Caterpillar thinks is the end,
the Butterfly knows is just the beginning."
~ Unknown Author

"It's never too late to live your happiest life."
~ Gayleen Williams

Today is the first day of the rest of your life. Begin now to live your happiest life. This quote by an unknown author expresses my sentiments so well, "Where we are today is a result of the choices we made yesterday. **Let's make the best choices today that we might have the best tomorrow."**

Happiness is no longer an "elusive butterfly." It's something you, too, deserve and can enjoy every day. Just as you use tools to build and maintain a house you can use your Happiness Action Tools™ to build and maintain your happiest life.

Henry David Thoreau shared this powerful quote, "If one advances confidently in the direction of his dreams, and endeavors to live the life which he has imagined, he will meet with a success unexpected in common hours."

You now know how you can transform into a beautiful butterfly flying free and happy! **Utilize your Happiness Action Tools™ so you can say:**

Positive Expectation Statement™

"I am living my happiest life!"

(8 words)

For free gifts to support you in being your happiest, visit your happiness community at TheHappinessCommunity.com.

APPENDIX A

A Few Words to Live By

- *"Life is a journey, not a destination."*
- *"We give power to people and circumstances when actually the power is in our own mind!"*
- *"This, too, in time shall pass!"*
- *"What's the worst thing that might (could) happen?*
- *"What would happen if...?" THEN: "What do I need to do now?"*
- *"We need to look for the gifts that can come from a negative situation, which may come in the form of reasons or lessons."*
- *"If we don't like a situation we have three choices: change it, move away from it or accept it."*
- *"There are no problems; only a creative challenge or opportunity."*
- *"When one door closes in life, a bigger and better one will open."*
- *"If you aim for a star you may only get half-way, but if you only aim half-way you may never get off the ground!"*
- *"We're all so busy 'BECOMING' when all we need to do is 'BE.'"*
- *"Life is for living — not crying or dying yet."*
- *"If you can see and feel yourself doing something in the theater of your mind then you can do it!"*
- *"Expect everything will take longer than you'd like it to. If it takes less time then you can be pleasantly surprised!"*
- *"If we think we can, we can. If we think we can't, we can't."*

For a printed copy of this page, please visit TheHappinessCommunity.com.

APPENDIX B

Positive Expectation Statements™

For the 21 Powerful Happiness Action Tools™

For Taking Action

"I enjoy taking effective positive action!" (6 words)

For Happiness Action Tool™ #1 - THE EFFECTIVENESS OF DECISIVENESS

"I now make effective decisions easily." (6 words)

For Happiness Action Tool™ #2 - THE ENERGY OF COURAGE

"I am now actively courageous in life." (7 words)

For Happiness Action Tool™ #3 - THE GIFT OF PURPOSE

"I live my life on purpose." (6 words)

For Happiness Action Tool™ #4 - THE IMPACT OF SELF-TALK

"I fill my head with positive thoughts." (7 words)

For Happiness Action Tool™ #5 - THE CLARITY OF FOCUS

"I consciously focus on being happy." (6 words)

For Happiness Action Tool™ #6 - THE POWER OF PERSPECITVE

"I approach life with positive expectancy." (6 words)

For Happiness Action Tool™ #7 -THE POTENCY OF ACCEPTANCE

"I fully accept everyone, including myself." (6 words)

For Happiness Action Tool™ #8 - THE VALUE OF ACKNOWLEDGMENT

"I fully acknowledge everyone, including me!" (6 words)

For Happiness Action Tool™ #9 -THE BLESSING OF FORGIVENESS

"I fully forgive everyone, including me." (6 words)

For Happiness Action Tool™ #10 - THE MIRACLE OF GRATEFULNESS

"I find much to be grateful for everyday." (8 words)

POSITIVE EXPECTATION STATEMENTS™

For the Happiness Action Tool™ #11 - THE SPLENDOR OF GENEROSITY

"I now delight in giving and sharing." (7 words)

For Happiness Action Tool™ #12 - THE SIGNIFICANCE OF TRUST

"I trust the process of life." (6 words)

For Happiness Action Tool™ #13 - THE STRENGTH OF INTEGRITY

"My actions reflect my best self." (6 words)

For Happiness Action Tool™ #14 - THE BENEFIT OF ORGANIZATION

"I enjoy the benefits of being organized." (7 words)

For Happiness Action Tool™ #15 - THE GENIUS OF CREATIVITY

"I enjoy allowing my creative genius." (6 words)

For Happiness Action Tool™ #16 - THE WONDER OF IMAGINATION

"I enhance my life with imagination." (6 words)

For Happiness Action Tool™ #17 - THE ASSET OF PERSEVERANCE

"I keep at it until I get it" (8 words)

For Happiness Action Tool™ #18 – THE INSURANCE OF SELF-DEVELOPMENT

"I now enjoy adding to my knowledge." (7 words)

For Happiness Action Tool™ #19 -THE ASSURANCE OF SUPPORT

"I surround myself with positive people." (6 words)

For Happiness Action Tool™ #20 - THE MERIT OF ENTHUSIASM

"I seize the day with enthusiasm." (6 words)

For Happiness Action Tool™ #21 - THE TREASURE OF PLAY

"I enjoy the treasure of play." (6 words)

APPENDIX C

Your Free Bonuses

The Happiness Community

To assist you in staying your happiest, we are giving you several powerful bonuses. Please visit TheHappinessCommunity.com to activate your **free membership** in the club designed to support you in building your best life and being your happiest. There you will find many gifts, including:

- An e-book of quotes for each Happiness Action Tool™
- A printable list of Positive Expectation Statements™ for each Happiness Action Tool™
- Printable version of "Words to Live By"
- David Stearn's cartoons of The Cosmic Waverider, some without color, allowing children to color them in while learning valuable lessons
- Many inspirational poems and stories from multiple sources, available in PDF format for printing
- Many books and products you can purchase for gifts and/or use in living your happiest life
- A forum for you to share your experience and get to know other Happiness Community members

As a member, you will receive invitations to seminars, webinars, and other happiness events with special member benefits, as well as discounts on products and/or services.

Check back often, as this site is a love-in-progress™. We will be continually updating it and adding valuable content so you can truly live your happiest life.

Dedication

I dedicate this book to David Stearns, my brother. He kept it alive over the years with his questions from the proposed table of contents and the beginning of a couple of chapters. Its completion is primarily due to his encouragement. He has been there for me, often with little notice, so many times I cannot count. I could never repay him for his generosity, kindness, love and time.

David doesn't mind me sharing that he has been diagnosed as bi-polar. He wrote the following poem after I separated from my husband, and I was at a very low point in my life. He wrote it to tell me how much my then **unfinished** book had helped him. I have seen such growth in him; and reading this poem I knew then I had to finish my book, both for him and for myself. Thank you, David. Your health is my reward. I am very pleased to say David is doing better than ever. He is so well balanced and happier than most people I know! He has come to such a place of peace with himself and his life that he is an inspiration to me.

David's creativity is also expressed in a cartoon series. His leading character is Trosein, aka "The Cosmic Wave Rider" who can ride water waves, sound waves, and light waves – and happiness waves!

DEDICATION

Getting Better

I'll try to explain how I feel
You walk me through this world;
You make it real.

The brightness of life in my view
I now see sunshine for its hue:
That life is alive and worth living,
This is how I feel about your giving.

Substance to relationships and positive effect
Virtue and value are esteem to get.
No one knows how confused I've been.
Life matters. It is worth living again!
Credit to activity, it is worth doing.
The habit of accomplishment, brewing
Noting what is of value and remembering it.
Knowing that it is valuable and worth giving it.

Maybe now you feel a little set back,
However, what you've done for me
Is give me life I never had.

Over the years you've cared for me
When the burden was great
You were more than a sister; you were motherly.

Now that I've grown and have to face life
Your guidance helped me decide to do right.
When I've found it hard to be me
I was helped by your mission of self-esteem.

By David G. Stearns © 2005

DEDICATION

I also dedicate this book to our mother, Mary June Stearns, who passed away in 1988. She was not just my mother she was my best friend. I still miss her, yet I know anytime I want to talk to her I can hear her words of wisdom in my mind. She has become one of my "friends of the mind," as the famed speaker and author, Dottie Walters, referred to them.

When I was 17 years old, I ran away from home. Now, I only went across town to my grandmother's, yet my mother missed me so much she wrote a beautiful poem about me being a butterfly lost somewhere between her heart and her imagination. It seems appropriate to include a copy of her poem with this book. The butterfly you see throughout this book is in her honor. It represents the renewal process; something she believed was always possible.

My mother was such an inspiration to me. Even though we were very poor she always told me I would go to college, so I never, ever, considered that might not be possible. Many of the "A Few Words to Live By" (*Appendix A*) were my mother's words. She taught me to believe in the possibilities.

How ironic that she named me Gay Kathleen – or maybe not. She wanted me to be happy, and she was a great visionary. As an adult, in expressing my individuality, I combined my first name and middle name to form the name Gayleen I go by now. I can see her in my mind's eye now, looking down on me from heaven and smiling. Her vision for my happiness held fast and has manifested in my life, most openly evidenced in my authoring this book!

She dearly loved books and would have loved to have owned a bookstore. She'd be so proud of her daughter, the author.

DEDICATION

A Pair of Butterfly Wings

Have you seen them?
I lost them somewhere,
Between my heart and my imagination.

They were a shimmering blue,
With tiny specks of gold.
So fragile – that to touch –
The velvet would flake on your finger.

And yet they were so strong
They could lift you to the sky
To soar among the beautiful trees
And to look at the golden earth below.

Oh have you seen my wings?
I seem to have lost them somewhere
Between my heart and my imagination.

By Mary June Stearns © 1966

Acknowledgments

I love this quote from an unknown author, "Some people come into our lives and quickly go. Some people move our souls to dance. They awaken us to new understanding with the passing whisper of their wisdom. Some people make the sky more beautiful to gaze upon. They stay in our lives for awhile, leave footprints on our hearts and we are never, ever the same."

It would be impossible for me to acknowledge all of the people who "left footprints on my heart." Many people's actions I'm sure I don't remember and I'm sure there are some I did not know their value. That being said, I would like to acknowledge the following people.

I would like to acknowledge Dell Morgan, for her monetary generosity and her attention to detail.

Linda Grau has been my friend and staunch supporter for longer than either of us care to admit. Her enthusiasm about this project, helped fuel its existence and completion.

Kay Reul is a very dear friend who definitely needs acknowledgement. She has shown an unswerving belief in me and has supported me through many life challenges. I really appreciate both her enthusiasm for this book and her inspirational ideas.

Carol Latham was involved in the conceptualization of this book. Her gentle nudging over the years contributed to its completion.

Dr. David Sauber is responsible for the first thought of this being a book. It was at his prompting that I changed my focus from writing the information as a seminar. (I have lost touch with David, who lived in Los Angeles, California at the time, so if anyone knows his whereabouts please ask him to contact me. Thank you.)

ACKNOWLEDGEMENTS

Patricia Clason, RCC, the owner of Accountability Coaching Associates and Director of Center for Creative Learning, was an inspiration to beginning this book. Encouragement from a woman of her stature helped me believe it was truly possible and had merit.

I want to acknowledge Ernest Stewart and John Hobgood whose loyal friendships helped save my life at a very traumatic time. Ernest's wife, Kimberly Stewart, is now also a wonderful addition to my life as a trusted friend.

My high school counselor, Mary Jo Weidman was one of the first people to see and encourage my leadership potential as well as listening and helping me dry my emotional teenage eyes.

With the guidance of Sharon Kay Prenzlow, my psychological counselor years ago, I gained a deeper understanding of myself, and how my life experiences affected the outcome of my life. Thank you so much Sharon!

Many other people have supported me over the years through my creative challenges. I would especially like to thank Rosemeri Ciliberto, Chris Bowser and Elaine Vener, all long-time friends.

Rhonda Frascelli's encouragement kept me going many times. Debrah Amad's honest critiques have added true value. Julianne Tozar's "way with words" was a big help "just when I need it."

If I missed someone, please forgive me. I am truly blessed to have so many wonderful people in my life.

Thank heavens for Marisa Stewart's eye for detail! Trust me if there are any errors in here it's my fault, not hers!

Last but certainly not least, I must acknowledge my writing partner (and friend) Linda Hancock Moore who put her own book on hold to help with mine. Thank you so much, Linda. My book is more powerful for your expert, yet intuitive and heartfelt, input.

Index

INDEX

INDEX

INDEX

INDEX

INDEX

INDEX

INDEX

INDEX

INDEX

ABOUT THE AUTHOR

Who is Gayleen?

Gayleen Williams radiates confidence and happiness. She speaks from her heart and her life experiences sharing how anyone can be happy most of the time.

Gayleen has led an interesting and yet challenging life, one that has had a lot of heartaches and disappointments. Coming from a background of poverty, dysfunction, and sexual abuse she spent many years feeling unhappy, discouraged, overwhelmed and exhausted. During many years of research, she found empowering Happiness Action Tools she began to use, and still does. Now she has a sense of well-being, is energized, enthusiastic and happy almost all the time!

Her creative and entrepreneurial spirit led to a diverse personal and professional life. She married three times and is proud that she stayed friends with all of them. The only thing she regrets is that she was never blessed with children. She is proud to have been a "second mother" to her three younger brothers while their mother worked to support them single-handedly.

Gayleen is now a Happiness Coach, Author of this book, and a Public Speaker. Gayleen holds numerous certifications in the area of personal development, including Life Results Coach, Hypnotherapist, and Neurological Repatterning Practitioner. She was also a Licensed California Real Estate Agent and has an AA Degree in Interior Design. However, the degree she is the most proud of is her "Degree in Happiness."

She refers to herself an "information junkie," which explains why she has also done a lot of independent study, along with attending a wide variety of classes, lectures, seminars and workshops.

ABOUT THE AUTHOR

One of her creative careers was ownership of a design business, which included architectural design of custom homes, interior home design and teaching interior design. This led to her founding a professional interior/architectural trade membership association, which included a referral service, a quarterly full-color high-gloss magazine and trade seminars. She published the official directory for an industry trade show and coordinated the line-up of expert seminars for that event. Because of her reputation in the industry, she was the featured speaker at a number of professional organization meetings.

She held a national record for over ten years for the single largest sale, both in dollar volume and number of units sold, for Hickory Farms. As a Director for PrePaid Legal, she had a sales team of over 4,000 people.

Gayleen worked as a legal secretary for four years while her mother battled cancer. She is proud to have been the assistant to the head of litigation, who was also on the four man executive committee for the prestigious national law firm. She also worked for the senior managing partner of the prestigious firm.

Working in conjunction with the Beverly Hills Chamber of Commerce she sold advertising for their City Directory and launched their first Christmas retail publication; single-handedly selling almost every ad in the magazine. As an advertising consultant, she represented many respected regional publications.

She also formed a company selling cosmetics and skincare. This let her express her creativity as a make-up artist and allowed her to offer her gift of enhancing people's self-esteem and happiness.

Gayleen now spends her time creating website and graphic design projects as well as writing and promoting her books. She is living her purpose, filled with passion.

Gayleen still experiences human emotions, such as sadness and anger. However, she manages to refocus herself and get back to happiness and a state of joyful expectation quickly now. No wonder Gayleen is often called "HAPPY GAYLEEN!"

ABOUT THE CO-AUTHOR

Who is Linda?

Linda Hancock Moore is a gifted wordsmith. She can add richness to an ordinary sentence and make it sing with interest. She loves both books and film, and although she enjoys every genre, she especially resonates to that which gives joy and raises consciousness, which is evidenced soulfully in her contributions to this book, *THE HAPPINESS TOOLKIT*!

As Gayleen Williams, original author of this book, put it, "Linda began as an editor; a very creative editor for the book, but her wonderful writing talent and creativity, coupled with her sincere enthusiasm and passion for the message, has made her contribution much more significant than that of an editor. She is more deserving of the title co-author, and I'm happy to share it with her."

Linda has had a life-long passion for film, which compliments her writing endeavors. For the past several years, she has assisted others in perfecting their writings all the while quietly working on her own. She has a natural understanding of the intricate workings of the creative process, the part that gives life to the art itself, as well as having a keen sense for the underlying motivation of those who aspire to create it.

In her early adult life, Linda found herself a single mother with a much-loved little girl. Wanting and needing to support the two of them, she used her creative side and her strong entrepreneurial side together, to build, own and operate four daycare centers, nurturing hundreds of children. Loving to travel and always seeking to experience new things led her to become an international flight attendant. Later retiring from the skies, she became a partner in an employment agency in Long Beach, California. All of these experiences honed her people skills, giving her a deep appreciation of life and a diversity of experience that serves as an unlimited source to draw from for her creative endeavors. At this point on the path, she sees her purpose clearly, and is now living that purpose by sharing her life experiences in her writings, adding happiness to the lives of others, while getting happier in her own.

Linda is excited to be moving back to California so she can be near her grandson who just got a recording contract! She spent the last several years living in Dallas, Texas so she could be near her now grown daughter, who she continues to learn from, a son-in-law she is proud of and her three grandchildren, who she refers to as "delicious." Now, that's a word only a creative writer – (oh excuse me) author - would think to use.

Like this Book?

THE HAPPINESS BOOK is available for purchase of single copies or in quantity. You can also contact us to discuss the option of customizing the book with the addition of your company name and/or logo on the cover.

Ideas for use:

- **As a Textbook** or other curricula for learning
- **As a Thank You Gift** to clients to insure customer loyalty
- **As an Employee Gift** increasing ROI by increasing productivity, retention, less absenteeism, safety and more
- **As a Sales Incentive/Premium**
    - Free with purchase
    - For visiting your store/company
    - For a sales appointment
    - For opening a new account
- **For completing a Survey**
- **Association Giveaways**
- **Free Drawing Prizes**
- **Trade Show Giveaways**
- **Referral Generators**
- **Value-Added Bonus** included with product or invoice
- **As a Fundraising Vehicle**

Workshops, speaking engagements, webinars available.

Published by:

Butterfly Publications

800.890.0996

ButterrflyPublications.com

email: support@ButterflyPublications.com

www.ingramcontent.com/pod-product-compliance
Lightning Source LLC
Chambersburg PA
CBHW072120270326
41931CB00010B/1616

* 9 7 8 1 8 9 2 6 4 4 3 1 2 *